THE
INTENTIONAL
MBA

THE
INTENTIONAL
MBA

A GUIDE TO MAXIMIZING YOUR
DECISION, EXPERIENCE AND INVESTMENT

CHRISTINE DAGENAIS, MBA, PCC
AND **RENÉE FRANCIS**, MBA

 FriesenPress

Suite 300 - 990 Fort St
Victoria, BC, V8V 3K2
Canada

www.friesenpress.com

ISBN
978-1-5255-2984-9 (Hardcover)
978-1-5255-2985-6 (Paperback)
978-1-5255-2986-3 (eBook)

1. BUSINESS & ECONOMICS, CAREERS

Distributed to the trade by The Ingram Book Company

Hello.

This book is dedicated to you and your curiosity.

Here's to your MBA exploration,

and may you enjoy many happy returns.

Acknowledgements

We could not have made this book without the enthusiastic and loving support of our husbands, Kyle and Wilco. Thank you both for the encouragement, proof reading, brainstorming, domain purchasing skills, and patience.

Our communities make us whole, and the same is true for the process of writing this book. To our colleagues, friends, and family, we are grateful to you for your considered and thoughtful feedback, told with loving honesty. This book was possible because of your input.

We also thank each other for a fantastic partnership and recognize what a journey this has been for us. The timing of writing this book has run in parallel to the busiest periods we've encountered in our careers and lives, and there have been a lot of late nights and early mornings to get here. We worked diligently from the outset of this project to be exemplary MBAs, intentionally applying what we learned in our MBA experiences at every opportunity. This has been a great adventure.

Table of Contents

Introduction

This book is for anyone considering a Master of Business Administration (MBA) program, hoping for a maximum return on their investment (a.k.a. ROI), and looking at an MBA experience as an opportunity for a significant life change. They are likely someone already engaged in their career and looking at a program that allows them to continue to work full time while they study. This is typically an Executive MBA (EMBA) program, though there are several types of programs out there.

As we wrote this book, we had the potential student and current student in mind, but no matter where you are in your decision or studies, you will find information here to help you get the most out of your MBA experience.

The Intentional MBA is also for MBA graduates whose convocation day has come and gone. We believe it's never too late to get the full return on your MBA investment by revisiting some of the most important aspects of your experience.

This book is written for MBAs by MBAs.

How to use *The Intentional MBA* and what to expect

Our goal is to provide a guide to help you create your very own intentional MBA experience to maximize your investment and to define and achieve your ROI. By creating an intentional MBA, we mean being mindful and purposeful in using your skills of observation to take in information and respond in the most thoughtful way. Creating an intentional MBA is about actively choosing, being fully invested, not wasting any moment, and being the most efficient participant in every experience.

Each chapter has valuable action tips or exercises to work through in service of these goals. This book is intended to be carried around with you, so you can easily create meaningful actions for yourself by writing directly in it.

Or, consider starting a folder on your computer, phone, or tablet where you can keep all your mindful MBA activities in one place. Download a reflection app or one that makes taking and tracking your notes easy. A simple spreadsheet will also work if that's your style. Or go analog with a cool journal to hold your journey.

Whatever you do, find a way to record your progress and thoughts that works for you. The right way to record your progress is the method you use. Before you know it, you'll have become mindful of your intentions to shape your MBA experience.

The Intentional MBA has six components, with a chapter dedicated to each component:

1. **Get ready:** Deciding, preparing, and bringing your intention

2. **Myths:** Clearing up misperceptions to ease your mind

3. **Planning:** Preparing to be intentional and gathering support

4. **Purpose and presence:** Maintaining mindfulness and intention throughout
5. **Learning:** Going beyond the curriculum
6. **Maintaining skills:** Keeping your intention beyond graduation

Whether you are reading this before, during, or after your MBA experience, we are confident you'll find useful information in each of the chapters. Start at the beginning and read it chapter by chapter, or go directly to a specific chapter that is most relevant to you at any particular time.

See yourself in these pages

Whether you're considering an MBA, studying deeply at this very moment, or looking back on your MBA from the perspective of years gone by, we believe now is the right time to get the full return on your MBA investment. Throughout the book, we'll apply the concepts through the experiences of three people: Jessica, Mohammed, and Leena, who each represent a phase of the MBA experience.

Think of Jessica, Mohammed, and Leena as your intentional MBA guides; examples of what the application of being intentional in your MBA journey might look like in your real life. Our fictional guides won't be exactly like you, but they approximate general representations of what we see in the pre-, during-, and post-MBA experience. We trust you can use their experiences to see yourself in these pages.

Pre MBA – Meet Jessica, age twenty-eight, marketing manager and aspiring entrepreneur who wants to grow her business

Jessica works during the day as a marketing manager for a large organization, where she has been for four years. She loves her work and is still learning and growing professionally. However, her true passion is her side hustle, a blossoming online business where she helps entrepreneurs bring their ideas for apps and web applications to life through project management and stakeholder engagement. She is excited about the companies and industries she's been able to do this work with.

Jessica has a lot of ambition to grow personally and professionally. She would like to shift her work away from a corporate-marketing job entirely and toward running her own business in app and web-based design and consulting. Jessica is outgoing and energetic, and confident in her ability to sell an idea. But she is unsure of how to manage the financial aspects of her own company and build a sustainable business. She's been in the industry for a long time and has a network of all the right types of services needed to design and launch a successful app. She's realized app development is truly a niche in today's evolving business environment. Her app clients have been growing through word of mouth, and Jessica is getting busier with work she truly loves, but she is not spending time on developing the business itself.

In some ways, Jessica has a ton of freedom. She doesn't have kids or a significant other. In other ways, she feels there's no way she could pay to do an MBA to learn how to transition her career toward her entrepreneurial dreams, build a business, and be successful in the long term. She already feels like all she does is work, with her only free time being an hour at the gym when she can make it. Where would she find the time? Jessica wants to invest in her future but can't see how to do that.

During an MBA – Meet Mohammed, age thirty-nine, a mechanical engineer who doesn't want to be pinned to the same job for the next fifteen years

As he looks ahead to his fortieth birthday, Mohammed is feeling his age. He is tired from pulling long days at work and keeping up with his first-year studies in an Executive MBA program. All his free time is dedicated to spending time with his wife and three active kids, but that time is limited due to the demands of his MBA program. When he's not studying or working on team assignments, he can be found shuttling his kids to and from their various activities, and he does so happily because his family is important to him.

With his family's well-being and future in mind, he aspires to do more with his career than the technical roles he's been in since he graduated with his engineering degree. Mohammed would like to be a non-technical leader, the kind who inspires his team and drives vision and strategy. He aspires to develop strong leadership capabilities and needs help to find ways to get out of the MBA all that he hopes he can.

Mohammed is worried that rather than managing to put his energy into the courses and assignments in his MBA program that will help him to reach his leadership goals, he'll end up reverting back to his expertise and take on all the group projects related to his technical skill set (quantitative, analytical) where he knows he can get an A+. He needs motivation, support, and lots of ideas to be held accountable to why he decided to do an MBA at such a busy time in his life. Mohammed is a little shy and lacks confidence when it comes to networking and talking about his transferable skills.

 ### Post MBA – Meet Leena, age fifty, a vice-president of asset integrity who feels stuck

Leena graduated from her MBA program two years ago, but hasn't since made a role change. She's been at an energy company for six years and has always worked in the energy industry. After having earned numerous promotions in the early stages of her career, Leena now feels stalled. This is especially frustrating because with her newly empty nest at home, she has the energy and experience to dedicate to reaching her goal of working at a chief executive level.

Leena worries about whether she's put her MBA experience and credentials to the best use and if she should switch industries to make her goals a reality. She is used to being deemed "top talent" and a "high potential" and is not feeling that she is operating at her full capability or capacity in her current role. She is ready for the next challenge but doesn't know where to start.

Over the past six years, the job market has changed significantly, and Leena is not aware of the best way to pivot in a career. Additionally, she is unsure of trying something new because she's always been in the energy industry focused on asset integrity. Her network is limited to those in her company, as she hasn't needed a network outside of work. Her aspirations for more are getting clearer every day, with her motivation increasing in parallel. It's time to be intentional about leveraging her MBA to achieve the desired next step in her career.

Why we wrote *The Intentional MBA*

We, Christine and Renée, share a love of learning and adventure. Collaborating on a practical handbook for MBAs during their education and in their later business life is a way for us to help MBAs get the most of their experience, a goal we're both intensely passionate about. We believe an MBA experience, when approached mindfully and with intention, can be a transformative and rich process. Getting an MBA can be the simple collection of three letters after your name, or it can be a personal and professional game changer. We are on Team Game Changer and are inspired by sharing actionable, easy, and productive ways to get the maximum return on your MBA investment.

Serving others by offering value and helping people reach their highest potential is close to our hearts, personally and professionally.

You'll read more in Chapter 6 about how to introduce yourself in a new way, something we call the instant credibility statement. We'd like to introduce ourselves to you now, in that format:

Hi, my name is Christine Dagenais, and I'm the Founder and CEO of Bright Wire, a premier leadership development and executive coaching firm in Canada. I am a certified professional Executive Coach and am also the co-author of the newly released book, The Intentional MBA: A Guide to Maximizing your Decision, Experience, and Investment.

I lead a team of Calgary's best executive coaches and leadership development experts in helping our clients discover possibilities that didn't exist for them prior to working with us. Through one-to-one and team coaching, as well as leadership development strategy consulting and the design and delivery of leadership development programs, we help clients achieve their personal, organizational, and professional goals, be it enhanced leadership capability and/or greater business results.

I love what I do because my work allows me to take my seventeen years of related experience, my graduate degree in business, and numerous leadership-training accreditations to translate the softer side of learning and leadership development into tangible results. I have become known for my ability to listen and quickly synthesize, to lead a strong team, to drive performance for our clients and for bringing innovative approaches to individual and corporate leadership development. The success of our clients and that of my team is my reward.

I look forward to the opportunity to partner with you as you continue to develop your personal and professional leadership capabilities, and become intentional about what you want to create for your future.

Hello, I'm Renée Francis, co-author of this book you're holding. I'm a strategic communications professional and experienced leader. I lead teams of ace corporate communicators to achieve their very best by creating a positive team environment and ensuring everyone can contribute. By combining active conversation with leadership teams with a deep understanding of all of the dynamic parts of a fast-moving *company and a view to the larger operating environment, I create targeted, effective corporate communications strategies. My work is about getting digestible and interesting pieces of information in the right places at the right times. All of this is in service of people, which includes customers, employees, and the communities businesses operate in, to create real business results.*

I love what I do because my work allows me to connect people with every aspect of what it takes for an organization to stay in business. Corporate information is fascinating to me. I love the challenge of making the stories of companies relevant. I believe when people can understand context and purpose, and how they fit into the big picture, everything is possible.

Businesses are filled with unique people, factors of both failure and success, and challenges. I want to understand all of it and champion those I work with to shine their brightest. This passion led me to build on my background in communications with a Master of Business Administration degree.

Mostly, I just love sharing words with others. When writers enjoy the words they write, readers feel it, and they enjoy reading. I hope that's your experience with this book, and thank you for reading it.

We believe that small, intentional practices of self-reflection and application can have a large, measurable impact on your career, MBA experience, and outlook on life. Our book is written as your guide to making your best decision and getting the greatest return on your MBA experience.

Chapter 1
Get ready: Deciding, preparing, and bringing your intention

How do we measure our investment?

As far as business jargon goes, ROI must be a chart-topping hit in the financial and business world. A close cousin to ROI in business jargon is "bang for your buck". Of course, ROI is an actual formula (*gain from the investment - cost of the investment ÷ cost of the investment*). Things can get more complicated when you want to calculate ROIC, or return on invested capital, which can be calculated several different ways depending on your line of business and the factors you're measuring.

But let's not overcomplicate this. Jargon and complexity aside, the reason for ROI's enduring and broad popularity is because it measures the payoff of an activity. This evaluation is especially relevant when considering an MBA experience since it's an investment that must make a return, much like in the business world. Fundamentally, both businesses and people need to answer the question, "Is what I'm doing worth my effort? And if so, by how much?"

The answer to this very important question, as in all of life's biggest and best puzzlers, is that it depends. In the calculation of deciding your ROI for your MBA experience, you get to decide the inputs and the outcome. Your ROI should link to your goals for your MBA experience and reflect what you're mindful of in your investment as you work through the program (and even after you've completed your program).

One of the most common and tangible ways to calculate the ROI on an MBA is to use the classic ROI equation with your salary and the cost of the program (which could include other aspects of your total investment such as forgone income or other opportunity costs as a result of your studies) as your inputs (*salary increase - cost of the MBA investment ÷ cost of the MBA investment*). As you get promotions and your salary grows, your ROI will increase. Or, you can estimate how many years of salary increases are likely, relative to the costs of the program; in other words, calculating how many years it will take to recoup your costs or break even. These are solid, quantifiable ways to measure a return on an MBA.

But there's never just one way to measure ROI, and we don't think you should limit yourself to one measurement. Let's say that the skills you learn in your MBA allow you to do a deal differently or run a more effective merger, and you end up saving millions of dollars or implementing and completing it more quickly than you would have otherwise. In this kind of example, the ROI could be cost avoidance or efficiency rather than a salary or revenue increase.

Even less tangible, but not less valuable, is examining ROI in terms of personal satisfaction. A hugely successful return might be the self-fulfillment of taking on a challenge you once thought was impossible, such as being the first in your family with a graduate degree or pivoting in your career and moving to an entirely different role or sector. Personal satisfaction can be heavily based on your values and could include some personal recognition of pride, learning to learn again, building confidence, demonstrating tenacity or capability; whatever it might be that is fundamentally important to you, which you saw yourself strengthen and highlight through your experience.

One of the most significant ROI measures from an MBA experience can be the relationship development and relationship capital you build. Continuing to grow with a cohort or being in the ongoing good company of high-performing leaders can spark a limitless amount of catalyzing energy in your own life. Surrounding yourself with like-minded individuals to share success with can be an incredible support through life's biggest moments, career and otherwise. The exceptional friendships and professional relationships you can develop in an MBA program are intrinsically rewarding in vast and deep ways, and they can equate to future possibilities that often relate to financial and career advancement at some point in your future.

As frustrating as it can be that there is no one right answer to calculating whether or not doing an MBA is worth it to you, it's equally rewarding to figure out what *your* ROI is. Your ROI is the sweet spot of aligning your purpose and intention with the experience you choose to participate in during and after your MBA. It can and should consider all of the factors, qualitative and quantitative, that you hold as essential.

Jessica's personal ROI calculation:

Gain from the investment in her MBA = Skills to grow and scale web consulting business, opportunity to use her existing side hustle as a capstone project with input and feedback from professors, promotion opportunities in the marketing field, potential income increase of $40,000 per year if app business could be sole income source, ability to network with like-minded entrepreneurs, satisfaction of accomplishing a big challenge

Cost from the investment in her MBA = $84,000 tuition, 30 hours per week in class and for homework/group commitments, $18,000 per year in lost business for app consulting (due to having less time for side hustle), potentially less time to exercise, further limited time for friends

Jessica's ROI calculation is a mix of both monetary and non-monetary considerations. Her expected annual income gain after graduation is $40,000, and her costs include the total tuition amount for her program ($84,000) and the money she loses from diverting her energy away from her consulting business over two years while she studies ($36,000), which add up to $120,000. Here's a look at her monetary ROI calculation for her program, beginning the year after she graduates:

YEAR ONE ($40,000 - $120,000) ÷ $120,000 = -67%
YEAR TWO ($80,000 - $120,000) ÷ $120,000 = -33%
YEAR THREE ($120,000 - $120,000) ÷ $120,000 = 0%
YEAR FOUR ($160,000 - $120,000) ÷ $120,000 = 33%
YEAR FIVE ($200,000 - $120,000) ÷ $120,000 = 67%
YEAR SIX ($240,000 - $120,000) ÷ $120,000 = 100%

Looking at Jessica's monetary ROI calculation, she won't break even until her third year after graduation. At four years after graduation, Jessica sees a 33 percent monetary return on her investment.

It's important that Jessica weigh each of her monetary and non-monetary gain/cost considerations carefully, looking for what's most important to her and what are the realistic outcomes she can expect from getting her MBA. She estimates that by learning how to scale her web business, she will be able to earn $40,000 more per year than she currently does at her marketing job and her side hustle combined. It seems reasonable to Jessica that in four years, she will be on her way toward making up the two years of income lost or reduced that she will face by having to scale back her side hustle because of the demands of going to school.

Jessica remains worried about the time commitment of taking her MBA. Her social life is already on life support, and she worries about finding time to exercise, something she loves doing. However, when Jessica thinks about the chance to be her own boss and the pride she will feel about taking a risk like this, she gets excited.

"In the end, I decided that my key ROI measures were going to be the ability to build a business and become the entrepreneur I dream of. I am ready to invest the tuition and time to grow my business, even if that means stepping back from that work for the next couple of years. When I look back on this experience, I'll feel satisfied with my investment if I conquered this challenge, networked with other entrepreneurs, and had a solid business model ready to go," says Jessica.

Mindful and intentional throughout

No matter what, you must keep a calm mind before, during, and after your MBA experience. We need our minds for every activity we do, and yet it's so easy to become detached from this vibrant resource. By not fully using the power of our minds, we risk the ROI of an MBA experience (and, arguably, the ROI of all life's experiences) and that doesn't make good business sense. Business and mindfulness are not mutually exclusive; in fact, we believe the first cannot thrive as intensely without the last.

"Mindfulness is awareness, cultivated by paying attention in a sustained and particular way: on purpose, in the present moment, and non-judgmentally," according to Dr. Jon Kabbat-Zinn[1], a pioneer of mindfulness in the West. For many of our readers, this is about the point when they start to feel uncomfortable and the "hippy dippy alarm bells" start to ring. We get that. Let them ring for a few minutes and please come back to us. Maintaining your intention through your MBA is about remaining mindful of what you're doing and why.

As the alarms ring, you might be imagining the strain of a yoga class, seeing the serene faces of Buddha statues, smelling the wisps of incense, hearing chanting, and wriggling at the thought of having to meditate and be just that still. And maybe you're thinking that all of this is not quite your thing and you're here to find out about business anyway. We get that, too.

Mindfulness and intention can look like a lot of different things. You don't have to fit into a stereotype of what mindfulness may have been represented to you as, though being

1   As quoted in Camilla Sanderson's *The Mini Book of Mindfulness: Simple Meditation Practices to Help You Live in the Moment*. Running Press, Philadelphia PA, 2016

mindful may make you uncomfortable at times. And for the record, in the spirit of learning and growing, we highly recommend trying all things to see what fits for you. Go for the yoga class. Find a meditation practice. Sweat with others. Move with intention. It's with an open mind that we can truly expand and connect.

In the business world, choice, investment, and efficiency are critical, and these areas share vital territory with mindfulness and being intentional in all of our actions.

As you choose to go ahead, if you choose to go ahead (or look back if you've already graduated), make the decision to be immersed and present in your MBA experience. Be mindful of where you are and where you're going. Remember why you're taking an MBA to begin with, or why you once took an MBA. By simply being mindful, intentional, and purposeful in your journey, you have an opportunity to do so much more than just collect three letters. On this path, the small things really do add up to enhance your ROI today and for years to come.

Moment of truth – recognizing your first step toward an MBA

As you find your way to the MBA, choose to begin with deliberate intentions. For you to be successful, to thrive through and beyond an MBA experience, this path needs to have been your choice. If you're doing this for someone else, you will not enjoy it, and the road to success will be arduous. Worse, you reduce your chances of success. Do not simply accept a recommendation from someone else. You need your own compelling reason to commit to an MBA, and you need to make this choice intentionally.

For many of us considering an MBA, there's a distinct moment when we suddenly see things differently, and this moment starts our MBA journey because we choose to begin in another direction. We wonder what else is possible and how we'll make our success last. How have the past however-many years gone by so quickly, when at the same time so many things haven't changed in our careers? Either the shine on once-chosen careers and life paths is starting to fade, or sparks from unexpected sources are starting to smolder, throwing the paths we're on into question.

We call this the "moment of truth", and it's a tangible space in time when you're able to stand outside of your normal day-to-day life and see that you have the power of choice. This moment feels sudden, but it's been building slowly. You can recognize its approach by repeated doubts, questions, and shifts in perspective. We often push away thoughts that challenge how we're doing things, living our lives, and building our careers. But moments of truth persist until we face them and examine our thoughts thoroughly. As leaders, we may be used to having difficult conversations with others, and the moment of truth is about having the most difficult conversation with yourself.

For some, the moment of truth might be triggered by something exceptionally positive (like a marriage, promotion, or birth) or traumatic by nature (divorce, death, or loss of a job). Self-reflection, like a spotlight onto a mirror, is bright and powerful. The moment of truth is a vulnerable place, and this moment can either be uncomfortable or quite comfortable. Neither reaction to this vulnerability is wrong, and you have a choice to make your moment of truth meaningful.

When you make the moment of truth meaningful, it has the potential to be the anchor that makes your MBA journey a success. It will be the foundation you return to when things are difficult (because they will be) and your energy is lagging (because it will). This is the beginning of intentional choice.

If, in this moment right now, you're doubting the strength of your moment of truth, you may be saying to yourself:

> *Yeah, that's all well and good but it's not the right time for me to do my MBA.*

> *I'm not good enough. I won't get accepted anyway.*

> *I can't afford it.*

> *I'm too far along in my career, so it's not worth the investment.*

> *I'll be the oldest in my class.*

> *I won't be smart enough to hold my own in the program.*

> *I have a family, I'll never be able to manage all that I need to do.*

Take heart. These doubts are universal. Challenging your reality is tough work. You need to carefully assess the impact of this epic opportunity to develop yourself and what that means for you and those around you, including your personal and work relationships. This endeavour is expensive, but there's lots you can do to strengthen your application and increase your return on investment at many points along the journey. You can solve these temporary hurdles in front of your goal.

The moment of truth opens your curiosity and eventually helps you move forward to a place of confidence to see that you can create something that is just for yourself. It's that moment where the future has become clearer, and you now know what you need to do, or at least have clarity on the next step to take. You have a chance to change things right now, in this very moment. Circumstances don't need to guide you; you can create your own circumstances based on deep and honest reflection with yourself. This is what it feels like to be in your moment of truth – a moment of clarity and intention in decision-making. These are the decisions that often have significant impacts for your future.

At this point, focus on rallying for yourself. Rallying for yourself is exactly as it sounds – show up and cheer yourself on. (We describe what being your own biggest fan looks like on page 51.) Give yourself permission to make this investment of your resources, financial and otherwise. Don't wait for someone else to give you permission to do this. You have a strong reason for being here, and it's time to own it. You've been having tough conversations with yourself, and it's now about committing intentionally to the investment.

Action tip:
Define your moment of truth

If you're considering an MBA:

1. Articulate your commitment and reasons for doing an MBA. Practice framing this change of perspective for people who haven't been in your head, and work to be clear on what you intend to do and why.

2. Share your commitment and reasons with the key stakeholders in your life; the people you will need to make your MBA dreams happen. Pick these people carefully – select people who will actively listen and share honest feedback and support.

3. Reflect on how you feel about sharing this. What are the reactions and feedback you've received? Have you made assumptions? Were you surprised by reactions? This will test your commitment, so note what you respond to or feel defensive about. The goal is to feel more confident in your choice and to have meaningful discussions with those most important to you about a bold new path.

Jessica's moment of truth:

I've always loved a challenge and was raised to believe I can do whatever I put my mind to. My career in marketing has been incredibly rewarding so far, and the work I've done on the side to help clients build amazing apps has really brought all of my passions and skills into focus. I want to be a successful entrepreneur and know I will enjoy the challenging process of gaining the skills I need to build my business by going to school to earn my MBA. I see my future as a business owner, and this is an important part of building a sustainable future for myself.

If you're already on your MBA journey:

- How are you living and fulfilling your commitment to yourself as you work through this process? What are some examples of your commitment in action?

Mohammed's moment of truth:

Because I want to make sure I'm working outside of my comfort zone, I've asked my semester team to make sure that I'm the lead on our human resources projects, as well as on writing reports for economics. My default is to do the stuff I've always been good at – like calculations and making graphs. I'm happy to help my teammates who struggle with the mathematical side of things, so I've partnered with a classmate to help him with his Excel skills, and he helps me with writing skills. I've also asked my wife to check in with me regularly for encouragement and support to make sure I'm staying outside my comfort zone in my assignments.

I also want to grow my personal network, and I can be a little shy in this area. I thought it would be easier to focus on building my network one person at a time, so like my friend who struggles with Excel, I'm working with a few classmates in a one-on-one way to exchange strengths and challenges in each of my classes. Just asking them seemed awkward at first, but it's been nice to have someone to work with. I'm also getting to know my class better.

If you've graduated:

- Looking back to the reasons you earned your MBA, what does the evolution of your commitment look like today and are you satisfied? If not, what are you going to do differently?

Leena's moment of truth:

I completed my MBA because I wanted career autonomy, growth, and flexibility. I was challenged then by feeling like my opportunities were limited and that my career had stalled. I wanted to feel empowered to make the moves I wanted to make, to achieve what I know I'm capable of doing. I always worried about being seen as too eager. However, as I now reflect, I've overcorrected that fear, and as a result, I haven't applied my empowerment to make some deliberate and brave moves to change my role. I haven't even looked at roles outside of my industry as options. I'm going to make a plan to generate a wide range of options and get moving on things that give me autonomy, flexibility, and a promotion.

If you aren't sure you're in a moment of truth, you can inspire some moment-of-truth style reflection by considering:

- What's making me happy/energized/fulfilled right now?

- What feels uncomfortable/hard/directionless?
- What would I like to change in my career?
- What do I love about what I do?
- What do I wish I were recognized for?
- How are my goals and career aligned?
- What kind of leader do I want to be?
- What kind of leader am I today?
- How am I prepared for change?
- If I look back five years from now, what might I regret not doing today?
- What is my satisfaction comprised of? What are my conditions of satisfaction and are they being met in my life as of today?

According to the annual survey of the Association of International Graduate Admissions Consultants (AIGAC),[2] MBA candidates are looking at MBA programs for these top reasons:

63 % wanted to acquire new skills and knowledge about business

57 % were looking for access to job prospects, including the opportunity to transition into a new career

57 % wanted access to a strong network

42 % wanted the degree to increase their salary

41 % wanted the opportunity to advance a career within the same industry

41 % wanted to get or enhance their credentials

40 % pursued an MBA to make a positive difference in the world and to improve society

Christine's moment of truth:

The moment of truth came quickly for me, but became stronger and more clear over time. I was raised in a family where getting an education was never an option or if-type discussion. It was always, "When you go to university, where will you go and what will you study?"

After starting as an undergrad and then being shocked that four years could pass so quickly, I succumbed to my desire for continued

....

2   Edinburgh, Scott, Krithika Srinivasan, Andrea Sparrey, Scott Shrum, and Karthik Palaniappan. "2019 MBA Applicant Survey." 2019 MBA Applicant Survey, 2019.

learning by applying to the MBA program. But, the moment of truth wasn't the application itself because, in all honesty, the decision to actually pursue the MBA wasn't made yet. (I could always still decline the acceptance.) It was when I was actually accepted that I decided to jump in with two feet.

Unlike most Executive MBA students, I received verbal confirmation of my acceptance to the program. It was a Saturday in June, and I was meeting a colleague for a coffee at a trendy coffee bar downtown. As I walked in, I was tapped on the shoulder by the dean of the business school, whom I had met a few weeks prior for my interview. He proceeded to tell me I had been accepted into the program and that the letter would be arriving at my house any day.

Now that was my powerful, in-person moment of truth and a scenario that won't soon be forgotten. It forced me to come to terms with my decision to pursue an MBA, which was quickly translated to enthusiasm, pride, and gratitude.

Renée's moment of truth:

I had been given a great leadership opportunity and wanted to do more in that capacity. I also wanted to be the most qualified person the next time a promotion opportunity came around. At the same time, I wanted to contribute differently to the business and was feeling restless for a challenge. I wanted to know more about the most effective ways to run an organization and elevate people.

It was around this time that I started having those backyard, over-the-fence conversations with a new and friendly neighbour. We talked about business a lot, and he (himself an MBA) strongly encouraged me to look at pursuing an MBA. I could see his points about the value of an MBA and how it would align with my interests, but I was paralyzed by the thought of paying for it.

Without minimizing my very real concern over finances, my neighbour challenged me to think about what was possible if I wasn't worried about money. He said, "Money is a real thing. But it's not the only thing. You'll figure out how to pay for this if it matters to you. It shouldn't be the thing that stops you if you want this badly enough."

This changed my thinking and set me off to research a variety of programs and schools. That conversation was not only my moment of truth, but it was also the start of my own mindful, intentional, joyful journey through my MBA.

Career-path assessment model

We often make decisions around careers that are subjective and emotionally driven, or even unclear. Using this career-path assessment model applies a layer of objectivity to these important decisions. It will allow you to develop a sense of awareness around what you'll need to be happy in the next three to five years, so you can base your decisions on that.

When you have awareness of your conditions of satisfaction, you can focus the limited energy and attention you have on the career paths that are most likely to meet these conditions. This process helps you maximize your efforts for the greatest results by narrowing your focus on the career paths that would be most likely to provide you total career satisfaction. Finally, the model can be used to help make decisions between career options; be it job search, job offers, internal promotions, or cross-functional moves. To further refine your ideal career path and make effective career decisions, weigh your options using this model at every career junction before, during, and after your MBA program.

Start with column A, adding as many critical career criteria (or conditions of satisfaction) as you want. These criteria are the things you absolutely need to be totally satisfied and engaged with your career choices. Dream big, anchoring these criteria to what's most important to you. Discuss these criteria with a significant other or someone else close to you to be sure you don't leave anything out.

When working with clients in completing this assessment, Christine has seen great success by positioning the start of this exercise in this way: Imagine we are meeting for a coffee three years from now and I ask you how it is going with your career. You say to me, "Everything is excellent. I'm so happy in my job!" I respond with, "Well, that's so great to hear. Can you tell me what is in place for you in your job that makes you so happy? What is enabling your satisfaction in your role?"

Now, let's apply your responses to your actions today. Looking to your vision of the future, what are those conditions of satisfaction you describe? Whatever they may be (flexibility, empowerment, compensation, location, internal-development opportunities), write your responses down as your conditions of satisfaction (your critical career criteria).

Next, move to column B and add your current career and role as the option where things stay the same as they are today. Reflecting on your current career is important to establish a baseline from which to grow and develop and compare other career paths. Then, move across the columns adding the career options available or imaginable to you.

Consider as many options as you can, adding as many columns as you like. Consider careers that require your education or careers that will require your technical expertise. Consider careers that are similar to what you've done before, but in entirely new industries. Consider careers that don't ask for your education or experience, but could benefit from your transferrable skills (see the action tip in Chapter 6 to learn how to identify your transferrable skills).

When you think you've thought of every possible option, add at least two more. There are always more options than we initially consider. Asking a friend or trusted colleague for ideas if you're stuck can be helpful. For example, have you considered entrepreneurship? Management consulting? Working in a new industry using your education or working in the same industry in an entirely different function? Depending on how wide a net you want to cast, the career paths may be at the industry, company, or job-specific level. Don't limit your possibilities – this is the time to think big.

Now it's time to see how each career path ranks against your conditions of satisfaction. Take each career criterion and consider it against the related career paths. The question you want to ask yourself is, "To what degree will this career path meet my condition of satisfaction, based on what I know today?" Use a scale of one to five, five being very likely and one being not likely, and provide a rating for each.

It is important to acknowledge that you may not have enough insight to rate these paths without making some assumptions along the way. That's OK. It's still better to make an educated guess than to only use what you may be thinking today, which is likely to be entirely subjective. This process works well in helping separate logic from emotion to enable objectivity. Rate each career path based on what you know or can fairly guess at, and compare it to your base line. For example, would compensation at XYZ industry likely be higher (which gives it a higher score) or lower (which gives it a lower score) than your current industry?

You can do this by taking each of the criteria and working your way horizontally across, assessing each criterion across all optional paths, or by moving down the list of criteria within one path before moving to the next.

When you total the columns, the end result should be a quantitative assessment of which options should get most of your effort, highlighting a preferred situation or path among many. The criteria can be prioritized or weighted if you choose, but the total sum of the rankings tells you which career path is most likely to serve your career criteria and therefore suggests where you should spend your career search time.

The numbered rankings help introduce objectivity in your decision-making process. Let's say you are negotiating two job offers. You would compare both against your personal- ized career- path assessment model to validate each option's probability to meet your conditions of satisfaction. Doing so gives you a non-emotional perspective on your options, as well as greater confidence in your decision-making through an intentional analysis to make your decision (versus making a decision on only what you feel).

When you're thinking of the criteria you need for total career satisfaction and looking three years ahead, that time frame is important. (Using a horizon of five years would be the longest time frame we recommend.) Through our shared experience, we believe this time frame is long enough to allow you to imagine and plan a different reality, and not too far away that the unforeseen can get in the way of your imagining and planning. It's the perfect time frame to influence and create aspirations and to accomplish those objectives.

Here's the career-path assessment model (with examples to follow):

A **Career criteria** (The critical few things that you need to feel 100% satisfied and engaged in your role in 3 to 5 years.)	B **Status quo** (Your industry and role stay the same; rank where 5 is very likely and 1 is not likely.)
Criteria 1	
Criteria 2	
Criteria 3	
Criteria 4 etc. (There is no limit to the # of criteria.)	
Total scores	

New option 1 (Rank where 5 is very likely and 1 is not likely.)	**New option 2** (Rank where 5 is very likely and 1 is not likely.)	**New option 3** (Rank where 5 is very likely and 1 is not likely.)	**New option 4** (Rank where 5 is very likely and 1 is not likely.)

Here's an example of a completed career-path assessment model, where the option to choose a new role in a different industry yields the most likely result for attaining the selected career criteria:

A **Career criteria** (The critical few things that you need to feel 100% satisfied and engaged in your position in 3 to 5 years.)	B **Status quo** (Your industry and role stay the same; rank where 5 is very likely and 1 is not likely.)
Total compensation	1
Lead a team	5
Budgetary responsibilities	1
Positive corporate culture	5
Internal development opportunities	3
Flexibility with scheduling	5
Total scores	**20**

Be an independent consultant (Rank where 5 is very likely and 1 is not likely.)	**Work at firm ABC** (Rank where 5 is very likely and 1 is not likely.)	**Same role in current industry** (Rank where 5 is very likely and 1 is not likely.)	**New role in new industry** (Rank where 5 is very likely and 1 is not likely.)
5	4	3	4
4	3	5	4
3	5	1	5
4	3	2	5
5	3	4	5
2	4	3	5
23	**22**	**18**	**28**

Here's an example of Leena's completed career-path assessment model, after she decided to revisit her moment of truth for completing her MBA:

A **Career criteria** (The critical few things that you need to feel 100% satisfied and engaged in your position in 3 to 5 years.)	B **Status quo** (Your industry and role stay the same; rank where 5 is very likely and 1 is not likely.)
Attain c-level role	3
Earn top compensation in the industry	3
Work in a gender-balanced executive team	2
Less office politics/positive corporate culture	1
Challenges my skillset	2
Total scores	**11**

Join competitor energy firm in similar role (Rank where 5 is very likely and 1 is not likely.)	**Move to different area within current company** (Rank where 5 is very likely and 1 is not likely.)	**Similar role in utility industry** (Rank where 5 is very likely and 1 is not likely.)	**Similar role in government function** (Rank where 5 is very likely and 1 is not likely.)
5	2	3	4
4	3	3	3
5	3	4	3
5	5	5	3
4	4	4	2
23	**17**	**19**	**15**

Looking at her career-path assessment, Leena realized that the status quo could no longer be what she accepted. By staying where she was, she was getting the least of what was important to her. Worse, staying where she was would not allow her to honour the reasons she chose to earn an MBA in the first place. Leena's total scores strongly suggested she pursue a role at a competitor's firm as her highest priority (which had the highest score of 23 points) and in a similar role in the utility industry as her second priority (had the second-highest score of 19) because these two options have the highest probabilities of greater career satisfaction over the next three to five years. With this clarified perspective on her options, Leena began a plan to tap into her network to explore role options at her competitor's firm and with a utility company in the area.

Three essential considerations for an MBA program

With your moment of truth tucked in your back pocket, and your decision to take on the challenge of an MBA top of mind, it's now time to be methodical in your review of the criteria to consider as you take your next steps toward your goal. Clearly articulating your intention comes from considering three areas in this momentous decision: impacts to you personally, impacts to you professionally, and the school you choose.

As you visualize what's ahead, we'll also give you the straight goods on some common MBA myths. Consider this your MBA prep checklist and the last bit of due diligence before you get down to work. This is about managing your expectations and those of the people around you, on whom you are relying for support. When expectation and actual experience align, remarkable things are possible. Investing in the time now to explore your expectations with these criteria solidifies your intention and reinforces your moment of truth.

Essential consideration number one: Check the personal impacts

We can't say this enough: Make sure you are doing this for you. Your first task is to check in on your commitment to yourself. If you're not doing this because you want to, your ability to be successful is significantly at risk. You've got a lot of work ahead, much of it unrecognized since you will be the one logging long hours learning to work with new people on new challenges after you've already had a long day. Expect the unexpected projects, last-minute deadlines, personal emergencies, and emergencies that happen to your teammates to cause distractions and discontent at some point. This is the kind of work that only you will know you've put in and worked through, but it's the kind of work that matters a great deal to an intentional MBA. If you are not your number-one fan and seeing that work and knowing it matters to the end goal, you're making things unnecessarily difficult for yourself.

(We explain more on being your number-one fan on page 51 in Chapter 3 so you can start your own cheering section. And yes, it's going to feel weird at first to play this role, but know that sometimes your cheering section will only have you as a fan, so we think this is a good upfront investment.)

Are your friends and family ready for what's ahead? Go beyond the head-nodding type of conversation where people are trying to be generally supportive of your dreams. Have specific conversations where you outline what your friends and family will experience as people who love you alongside this journey, and what you can commit to during this time. Be realistic and honest. Set ground rules, and schedule time for the most important things (connection time, rest, exercise, birthdays, cooking, etc.).

Remember that you will also need some time to be alone and recharge, so plan for it. Where possible, set up some services to help lighten the domestic and personal task load. Consider meal and cleaning services, in-home massage, or a mechanic who will come to your house in the evening while you study. These services are worth their weight in gold when it comes to maintaining your sanity and health, as well as what you contribute to the household, all while avoiding resentment from the people you live with and increasing your probability of success in your MBA program. See more about assembling your personal network in Chapter 3.

Confirm that an MBA is right for you. Do one last check to ensure that an MBA is what you need for your career goals. An MBA allows you to acquire the latest business knowledge, trends, and practices out there, but it's a general degree and is not specialized. This can be appealing if you're specialized and want to generalize, as is the case with many professionals. Or, maybe you want to specialize further. There are lots of graduate-level options out there, and maybe pursuing an accounting designation, law school, or other specialized credential is more aligned with your short- and long-term goals.

An MBA is a generalist degree that will give you some excellent skills, but it's not the only answer to building the career of your dreams. This is your opportunity to do two years of graduate-level education, and it should fill the gaps you've identified in your skill set.

Essential consideration number one:
Personal impact checklist

☐ I really want to earn my MBA

☐ It's my choice to earn my MBA

☐ I can observe and appreciate the work I'm doing toward my MBA, even if no one else sees it

☐ I'm my number-one fan

☐ I've had honest conversations with my friends and family about what my schedule, commitments, and goals are

☐ I've got a plan to recharge my personal batteries

☐ An MBA program aligns with my career and personal goals

Essential consideration number two: Check the professional impacts

Add up the financial commitment and return. An MBA is an investment that requires considerable monetary resources, so you shouldn't take this investment lightly. Be realistic with yourself from the outset on how long you think it will take to get the return on your money and the time you'll invest in the program.

The monetary return of an MBA will differ for each person. It depends on your salary at the entry point of the program, on your overall goals, and on how your career changes through achieving those goals. Generally, your probability of a substantial increase in salary is higher if your salary is low, and lower if your salary is already high when you begin the program. However, from an entrepreneurial perspective, for example, the MBA could be where you generate or refine your biggest idea yet, allowing you to radically change what you were doing before with financial returns to match.

Regardless of where you begin, be realistic on what to expect and check in with your goals as well as your budget spreadsheet.

But remember the return is not all about money. As you will learn in a future finance class, the numbers are just the start of any business story. Consider the non-monetary benefits of doing an MBA, once again checking in with your personal reasons for committing to do this. For many MBA candidates, the most valuable parts of the MBA journey are increased self-confidence and the chance to create and belong to a high-powered network that extends locally or globally. Most MBA programs will have you going through the stages of team dynamics quickly and intensely, and you are likely to make lifelong friendships from these unique experiences. You're about to get into the trenches with strangers – expect that you'll come out the other side with bonds that run deep.

Learning to learn again is a challenge, but when you overcome the struggle, the benefits are refreshing. Discovering the joy of learning after many years away from school (several professional years of work are often required for admission into an Executive MBA program) adds energy to your work and changes your approach. Staleness just doesn't generate innovative ideas; the joy of learning opens opportunities and paths everywhere.

You don't have to graduate to start marketing yourself. As soon as you're enrolled in an MBA program, you are an MBA from a recruitment perspective. No, that doesn't mean you use the credentials right away. It does mean you state that you're enrolled with your expected graduation date. This demonstrates your commitment and trajectory, launching your return on investment from the start.

Essential consideration number two:
Professional impacts checklist

☐ Calculate your personal return on investment (ROI), including non-monetary benefits (see Jessica's example on page 14)

☐ Review your budget for tuition and other costs

☐ Review your time commitments for alignment with your current role and company's milestones (busy times, etc.)

☐ Consider your career trajectory potential

Essential consideration number three: What to consider in the school you choose

Location, location, location. For many MBA candidates, especially working professionals balancing full-time work, choosing a school comes down to where they want to develop their network and whether that network needs to be local or not.

What kind of experience and interaction do you want and need? Consider your learning style and personality. Do you want to be in a quiet room attending class by webinar? Or do you need a lively classroom to keep you engaged? Matching your personal preferences to the program's delivery is key to aligning your needs with the program's offering.

Consider the type of program delivery as well. For example, comparing an Executive MBA (EMBA) with a regular MBA program will reveal some crucial differences. EMBA programs typically run over weekends and intensive weeks to accommodate for the busy professional working a full-time job. You don't have to be an executive to enrol. These programs are tailored around demanding careers and study happening concurrently.

Regular MBA programs are offered in full- or part-time schedules where you can continue to work. However, there's a different level of experience and age in those cohorts, and you will find more work experience within an EMBA program's cohorts. If a senior-level network and experience are important to you, an EMBA program should be considered carefully.

University and business school's reputation

An MBA program is offered by the university's business school, and it's important to look at the reputation of both the university and the business school as part of your selection. In the 2019 Association of International Graduate Admissions Consultants (AIGAC)[3] survey of MBA applicants, 63 percent of respondents put a school's reputation and ranking as their top factors in school choice, with a school's culture (54 percent) and career impact (50 percent) as the next most important factors.

....

3   Edinburgh, Scott, Krithika Srinivasan, Andrea Sparrey, Scott Shrum, and Karthik Palaniappan. "2019 MBA Applicant Survey." 2019 MBA Applicant Survey, 2019.

Research what both the university and the business school are doing for investment, competitions, publications, etc., and forecast ten years ahead to what their ranking is likely to be. Are they scaling back or increasing their efforts to compete in the MBA landscape? Determine the probability of a degree from this school increasing in value or decreasing. If you're not clear about the direction the MBA programs are headed, ask the school and the faculty. If they can't give you some clear guidance on where the value of your degree will be, you don't want to go to that school.

Research and repeat

Ask a lot of questions, and make sure your questions reveal the value you need to get from your experience. If you have an undergrad degree from the same school you're considering for an MBA, you may want to look at a different school for diversification. Research the quality of professors in the program and the awards they've received. Teaching awards matter, so look at them for the kind of learning environment you're after. Just because someone has a PhD doesn't necessarily mean they are a good teacher, so evaluating teaching awards and the criteria that is part of those awards tells a lot about what to expect from the classroom.

Consider interviewing alumni over coffee, by video chat, through LinkedIn messages – any way you have available to you to connect directly with someone who has been there before. The strength of the alumni network will stay with you after the program, so ask what's available and where the opportunities are for ongoing learning and post-graduation programs. By talking with alumni, you can get a sense of what the long-term return on your investment can look like. We recommend choosing a school with a strong alumni program – it's an added benefit that brings value and fun. You will want ways to remain involved in the community. It's our experience that MBAs generally support each other first, and research has long shown that similarity draws people together.[4] Going to a school where a strong alumni community is already in place gives you an advantage.

Global exposure

Most MBA programs have an international component, and if this is important to you, be sure to look at what's on offer. Programs vary in how a global focus on international business is incorporated and may include content/curriculum, direct interaction abroad through international trips, and more, so find out what this component looks like.

Leadership

Look at the number of leadership courses the program offers. Of all the things MBAs are looking for, new leadership knowledge, skill development, and promotions top the lists. In most organizations, promotions require results achieved through others, a.k.a. effective leadership, and so lack of leadership knowledge and opportunities can often affect promotion. Learning and developing your leadership skillset, one that encompasses both the business and people aspects needed to advance, should be a key component of your intentional MBA journey.

....

4   Cialdini, Robert B. "Harnessing the Science of Persuasion." Harvard Business Review, October 2001.

Because leadership skills differentiate in business like no other skillset, it's understandable that they are highly sought after. However, not all MBA programs are created equally in this area – many are quite lacking in terms of providing students with leadership-focused experience and curriculum.

If you want to lead people better than you do today, look for a program that gives you a chance to practice this skill through the work. You can't just read about leadership to be a better leader. Ask what's on offer in the program and what the real chances are to put leadership into action. For example, are students assigned teams? What's the structure of those study teams, and can you play a leadership role in your program's study teams to apply the theory being taught as you work through the curriculum?

The finishing touches

Many EMBA programs offer an all-inclusive type of service. Because mature students have full lives and active careers, programs offer book delivery, parking, catered meals, etc. so students can keep their focus on the course work and networking. Be sure to evaluate what your program offers and look for the things that will make your journey a little easier.

Essential consideration number three:
School consideration checklist

- ☐ Location – where do you want to develop your network?
- ☐ What kind of experience and interaction do you want and need?
- ☐ Which kind of MBA program is right for you?

☐ Reputation research – what are the school and professors known for?

☐ Talk to alumni – what kind of experience did they have and how does it fit with your expectations?

☐ What is the global exposure of your program and how important is that to you?

☐ How will your program help you to become a better leader?

☐ What are the other perks or benefits of the program?

Chapter 2
Myths: Clearing up misperceptions to ease your mind

It's normal to be nervous. If you are asking yourself questions like:

Can I do this?

Am I good enough?

I haven't been in school for a long time; do I remember how to learn?

You are normal. These are frequent questions from adults re-entering the education system. We all experience self-doubt, even the most confident mortals among us. In fact, asking these questions demonstrates a healthy amount of nervousness and shows you care about something you're committed to. If you're *not* nervous, you might be setting yourself up for failure.

Don't worry if you're expecting this to be difficult; it will be. Manage your expectations on the upcoming challenge upfront. It's normal to be worried about volume and capacity. There is no perfect time to commit to doing an MBA. This will be a challenge and life's events will get in the way. And you should do it anyway.

The MBA journey is about learning what your full potential and full capacity could be and reaching a new level of accomplishment as a human being. Expect that things will get in the way, and expect that you will find a way through, becoming better in the process.

Myth:
With an MBA, I'll get an automatic promotion

We've all heard it before. "An MBA will make me automatically promotable." No, it won't. Often, MBA grads have a heightened sense of self-worth and exclusivity after they've completed the program, but three letters do not determine your promotability.

An MBA is absolutely a component of a goal to be promoted, but earning an MBA is not a guarantee you will get promoted. Your MBA will enable and help your next promotion, but it won't be the sole reason you are promoted. Promotion depends on merit, ability, capability, and potential. Think of earning your MBA as an important addition, not the whole promotion plan.

Myth:
An Executive MBA is basically a vacation

While we may want you to consider what's included in an EMBA program, an all-inclusive EMBA program is not like an all-inclusive vacation in a tropical place. An EMBA is not an easier program than a regular MBA program. The curriculum between the programs typically doesn't change. Rather, the EMBA experience is different and more convenient for someone who is working full time. The content and volume of an EMBA and regular MBA are no different, and some argue students have to work harder in an EMBA program because they're working full time while completing it.

Myth:
Talking about my MBA will give me instant credibility

This myth is risky at the best of times, so we recommend you approach this kind of thinking and talking with great caution. It's not that you can't talk about your MBA, the things you've learned, or your experience, but it comes down to how you say it and knowing the audience you say it to. What does your audience value? What adds to the conversation, and are you improving upon silence? An MBA alone is not enough to give you an instant credibility card, and you don't want to be overly aggressive because that will cause you to lose your audience before you've begun.

Go to Chapter 6 where we show you how and when to use your MBA credentials without sounding boastful. If you haven't already, head to Chapter 6 to create your instant credibility statement.

Christine says:

I coached a senior leader who was promoted to a VP-level position in a short period of time. Throughout the first month of his new position in a department new to him, he would introduce himself and be sure to share with the team all the credentials he had that qualified him for the role. This VP was an MBA, a professional project manager, and an engineer. The team did not require this information. They trusted him already because of the management team who hired him and, in fact, they were already aware of his very strong academic background. He made the mistake of assuming the team didn't know about his background and placed a high value on advertising his credentials. He led with that for too long, so much so that the team thought he was just a boastful person and came to find him annoying.

One day, a very courageous colleague said to this leader, "We all know you are capable and qualified. No need to tell us about your MBA anymore. We've seen the quality of your work and are behind you one hundred percent." The problem is that not everyone has a colleague brave enough to provide this feedback, so you want to mitigate creating this perception from the onset. From that day forward, my client scaled back his introduction and now keeps his education secondary unless he assesses it will prove beneficial, depending on the audience.

Myth:
An MBA will make my salary skyrocket

The trajectory of your salary after graduation depends on several factors. Your return on investment and your path to your maximum ROI as an MBA is up to you, and your salary increases will reflect your personal goals and specific situation. Before you begin your MBA, it's essential to consider your salary, the sector you work in, where you sit relative to others who do what you do, what you want to do next, and the local job market conditions.

If you begin an MBA with a low salary, chances are higher you will experience a salary increase. If you're the CEO and top-paid person at your company, you may see a lower percentage of salary increase or none at all. But remember, a salary increase may not be the measure of ROI for any particular graduate.

All that said, the *Financial Times* studies salary increases of MBAs and has generally found that MBA graduates from nearly all sectors experience an increase in salary three years after graduation.[5] In 2016, *Financial Times* found that alumni from their list of the top 100 MBA programs had increased their salaries by a little more than five percent from the previous cohort's average to an average salary of $142,000.

Keep in mind that program costs are generally rising, too, as are wages in many cases. To address this myth accurately and mindfully, you will need to survey your personal landscape carefully so you have a realistic expectation of your salary's trajectory.

. . . .

5   Ortmans Laurent, Moules Johathan. "MBA graduate salaries increase by record amount." Financial Times, January 29, 2017

Chapter 3
Planning: Preparing to be intentional and gathering support

How to become your own number-one fan

Would it be easier to put on one of those giant, brightly coloured foam fingers you'd find at a sporting event and cheer on a friend, colleague, or someone who reports to you than it would be to cheer on yourself? Does the thought of cheering yourself on make you uncomfortable? If you're reading that and nodding or wiggling in your seat, you're not alone.

For many of you considering an MBA, you may already be the type of leader who is known to champion others, advocating effectively for those you work with when it matters the most. This may even be a big reason and motivation for you to advance your career by completing an MBA.

The trouble is that most of us forget about ourselves or worry that if we do advocate for ourselves, we'll be seen as arrogant. Or worse, we believe that our work will simply speak for itself and that nothing but hard work is required. Your work may have, in fact, spoken for itself up to now, and you may have had excellent advocates up to now. However, the probability of this continuing to be true in today's competitive and fast-paced environment is low and shrinking.

Do not assume you will get credit where it's due. You have to put up your hand and be a little louder in the world today. It's noisy out there. A strong resumé with real, quantifiable results is not enough. The jobs go to those who follow up, make a connection, and are otherwise memorable. Others will not know who you are and what you do, so you need to tell them and showcase what you offer.

As you consider the leap to an MBA and getting the most from your MBA once you're done, it's definitely time to grab your own giant, brightly coloured foam finger and get used to advocating for yourself. It's time to be your own number-one fan. So show up and cheer yourself on.

Regardless of the pace and noise of the world, most MBAs will find themselves in situations where they have to position themselves in new ways and talk about how their skills and abilities differentiate them from others. After all, learning, growing, and being different than you were before are likely all part of your intention and purpose; your own carefully built ROI for doing your MBA in the first place. We hear all the time that people don't want to sell themselves or come across as selling something. Selling ourselves feels uncomfortable, and we get that. But if the people you're talking to don't know all that you've grown and become, how will they ever know if you don't tell them?

If we think of roles in an organization as being shaped like a pyramid, with the most senior roles at the top, that's precisely where supply and demand forces take stark effect. There's more demand for less supply of senior roles, and so the price of admission and acceptance goes up the higher you climb the pyramid. You need to be able to talk about yourself and why you are the best person for the top jobs; what your strengths are and why you are exceptional. Doing so is absolutely critical; this is exactly the point when you need to promote yourself the most. Even if others are sharing your good news, you have to be the foremost expert in your cheering section to get to the top.

The question is: How do you be your own number-one fan without arrogance? No one wants to scare away an employer or come across as a braggart (like the vice-president Christine worked with, because that was certainly not what he set out to do), but we all want to talk about what we've achieved and what we can do.

Being your own number-one fan can be genuine, and it can be comfortable, but it's going to take practice. You want your personal advocacy to be respectful and insightful, while leaving a clear message on what your contributions could be. Your advocacy and number-one fanship starts with your transferrable skills (see Chapter 6, page 146). Your skills are the path to getting confident about articulating what you do and how those skills relate to all kinds of situations.

When talking about your transferable skills, you want to aim for three to five skills that were likely present in all of your biggest successes in the recent past. Relevancy matters here, so keep your examples to the last three to five years. Reflect on the successes you've had in your life and ask yourself what you did that enabled that success. What were the skills you demonstrated in doing so? Chart your skills on page 150 in Chapter 6.

Using your instant credibility statement (that you will build in Chapter 6) is a critical start to building your confidence in speaking about your abilities in new situations. Remember that more often than not, you don't have time for your whole life story. Every one of us can fall into the default trap of talking about where you're from and all the stuff that's happened in between. Don't fall victim to that conversation trap; practicing your credibility statement will keep you on more effective conversational ground than telling a story about that time you travelled for a year after high school.

Removing arrogance from how you speak about yourself is rooted in being authentic. Just as we truthfully speak to our skills, we also remember what our gaps are and where there are opportunities for development. Be at peace with that. Self-knowledge and self-appreciation will only help you to adopt the mindset of a continual learner. Be OK about putting up your hand with that giant, brightly coloured foam finger and saying, "That's not my strength, but this is." Again, knowing your top three to five skills and how they contribute to your ongoing success is essential.

For the record, there's nothing wrong with building a network of champions who will represent you at the boardroom table and help you find your career path. In fact, we highly recommend it. It's just that you don't get to opt out of the advocacy work of being your own number-one fan by delegating this job entirely to your champions.

It's worth noting there's a big difference between mentors and sponsors in the world of your champions. As you get more confident in your own number-one fanship, you can ask for a sponsor, which is very different than a mentor.

A sponsor is an advocate for your career, someone who will put your name forward and make suggestions on your path to development or promotion. A sponsor is someone of influence whom you've specifically asked to be a sponsor. You've said, "Help me accomplish my career objectives, help me advocate so I have a better chance of influencing decision makers before positions are even posted," and that request has been granted. A sponsor has a tangible commitment to helping you fulfill your career objectives and operates in front of the scenes, not behind.

A mentor is a colleague, generally at a higher level than you, working behind the scenes of your career advancement, usually within your company. Mentors will help you navigate opportunities, while sharing their experiences and helping you to understand how the organization works. Mentors can help you manage and understand different procedures and practices, and they provide an ear to listen, usually in confidence, to help you understand. Mentors are those people you can create ideas with, and your meetings are typically not the kind that produce action items at the end.

Number-one fanship is really the art of combining these three sources of advocacy and recognizing that the first foam finger goes on your own hand.

Building a business case – customized preparation

Once you've lived your moment of truth and selected a program that fits your goals, it's now time to think about how to pay for the MBA program. If you're considering an Executive MBA (EMBA) program, or even a regular program, it's likely you'll continue to work full-time through the program. Considering the substantial costs of an MBA program, financing the tuition payment(s) and carving out the time needed to be successful is a significant and distinct part of your MBA journey.

Although this section is written for those seeking employer funding for their MBA, the business-case approach to creating a proposal outlined below is universal to many types of recommendations and pitches. Read on for some great ideas on how to structure your recommendations and future business cases, even if you are paying for your MBA yourself.

Building a business case for your employer to ask for full or partial tuition investment and the time away from work needed to complete your MBA is a critical step to making your MBA journey a reality. To convince your employer that an MBA is a strong investment, there are seven components you should include in a business case.

1. **Executive summary of your proposal**
2. **Return on investment (ROI) for the organization**
3. **Summary of your selected MBA program details at the highest level**
4. **Alignment to your career development**
5. **Financial structure and support requested**
6. **Work management plan**
7. **Appendix (optional)**

Documenting your strategy about how an MBA will evolve your skill set and enhance the skills you have is the story you need to be prepared to articulate to everyone you know before, during, and after your program. Presenting your business case also demonstrates serious and significant intention on your part, along with your commitment and loyalty, all of which are always valuable to document in a work environment.

Your business case will be as individual as you are, but getting it right will always involve customization and preparation. The best time to begin this work is yesterday; start sooner than you think you should, as you will likely learn and adapt through this process, and you will get more if you give yourself time to work through each step. Mastering your business case contributes to the durable foundation for your MBA journey. Remember that whether your business case is approved or not, even if your company hasn't invested in an employee this way before, it's worthwhile to put your case down on paper because it helps to hold you accountable to get the most of your MBA experience from start to finish and well beyond.

Seven steps to building a customized business case

In most organizations, for an investment of this size, at least a few steps and levels of approval are typically required. Your internal human-resources department may have a formal tuition-reimbursement program, so your first action is to complete your due diligence on whether MBA programs fall within the guidelines already in place. Many MBA programs are not eligible due to the cost, but that doesn't mean you'll stop the business case process. You just need to know the context of the environment in which you're pitching your case and the leaders who have influence in your organization.

Part of your environmental scan of the company you work for is knowing who you're writing your business case for and what the probability is of having it approved before you begin writing. Is there a precedent for paying for an MBA? What has been done before? Reach out to the people who have done this before you, including the leaders who may have supported those people. Consider that you may need to ask for permission to explore this topic before you even ask, and your human-resources department can offer guidance here.

Now, you're ready to begin. Tactically, your business case will have seven components that you will build based on your circumstances, and the result is a document that looks like a proposal with an executive summary. Here we will break down the seven components and how to tackle each.

1. Executive summary with your recommendation or proposal

This should be a basic format where you introduce the reader to what they're about to read and why this should matter to them. Keep it to one page, and include a small paragraph to capture what your reader can expect in each section of the report.

Consider including research or stats on the general value of an MBA, recognizing that the person reading this may not be familiar with what an MBA provides or may have an already determined impression that could even be negative about the value of an MBA.

Based on what Christine has seen through her coaching work with hundreds of leaders (many with MBAs), the value of many MBA programs is rooted in leadership capability and strategic thinking. These skills help students to discern complexity as they navigate through continued change and growth in an organization and the changing world around us. Additionally, an MBA experience requires an expansion of an individual's total capacity as MBAs find themselves having to do more with less time available. This expansion fosters greater time management and prioritization skills, not directly taught through MBA curriculum, but developed through the intensity of the experience. There is abundant information available about why MBA programs matter, so find a statement or two that fits with your expectations and with those of your reader (who is likely the person who needs to approve this request, a.k.a. your decision-maker).

It's also important to note that just because this is the first section of your business case, it should probably be the last thing you write since it's meant to summarize the other components. If you must work from start to finish, at least begin with an outline and go back to update it when the whole document is done.

2. Return on investment (ROI) for the organization

Here, you will outline what your employer can expect from this benefit. It's critical to focus not on what you personally will get (because of course you will benefit); rather, focus on what the company can expect to achieve from this substantial investment in you.

If this is an EMBA program, you're probably doing this while working full time. One of the benefits of this kind of program, and a purpose you can highlight to your employer, is the opportunity of immediate application of the learning you'll be doing to the benefit of your daily work. Many projects will be focused on current employment, or certainly can be applied that way if you choose to. For example, in the program we (Christine and Renée) took, the first intensive week is a series of three papers that build to assess the management team of your current employer and their alignment to the company's vision. This information can be used right away to apply to the work students are doing.

Other benefits for an organization include more effective succession planning and talent management, which contribute to an overall business readiness. When one employee becomes a better leader, the bench strength of the whole leadership team is strengthened. Your company's presence in an MBA program enhances their presence in the business community and across industries, keeping skills and knowledge current. The ability to get this leading edge from working with and learning from your classmates is second to none.

By exposing yourself to different industries, paired with the latest academic knowledge, you may even be able to find opportunities where others, including competitors, may not see them. By investing in your education and knowledge, you're able to apply theory in new ways that provide innovation back to your organization.

Lastly, consider making the case for advanced education as a weapon in the fight against complacency. Regardless of the industry you're in, competition and market conditions demand agile learners who can adapt and anticipate. As your organization considers its future, it will want to fill its talent pipeline with leaders who've spent time practicing this set of skills.

This is not an exhaustive list of the return businesses can expect from an MBA investment. As with each component of your business case, this section should be customized to what matters for your organization. For this section, focus on highlighting how you will take opportunities to align the program's content to your work and drawing a clear link to your organization's benefit.

3. Summary of your selected MBA program details at the highest level

Here, you'll highlight why you chose the program you did and what the key features of that program are, ensuring you link back to how this reflects on or impacts your organization. Include the ranking of the school (consider sources such as *Financial Times, Maclean's, The Economist, Forbes,* etc.), since your company will want to align itself with a reputable school.

Give the details of the duration of the program, including start and end dates, as well as anything that makes your chosen program stand out. For example, list the specific courses you'll take, whether other benefits like coaching services are included, and if there is an international study/travel component. Note class sizes, etc., and if there are block or intensive weeks, a major project, or a speaker series where there is an opportunity for your company to participate. This section should also include the total cost of program investment, since you want to plant the seed here of what's estimated (your direct ask for funding will come later).

Lastly, be sure to include logistical details like application deadlines and how many days you expect to be away from the office.

4. Alignment to your career development

EMBA programs go by exceptionally quickly, and you will want to demonstrate that the pace and adaptability required to do this will accelerate the development you already have planned to benefit your organization. In this section, you are showing how you see yourself growing. Highlight how you will develop as a leader, noting what you expect to be able to work on and how that fits your organization's goals. Include the level and volume of challenge, as well as the long-term impacts to the role you play today and those you could play in the future.

For most, the MBA journey will now become your new and major investment in your development for the next few years. So, if that means there are no other conferences or training for the next two years, mention this and the condensed and controlled associated costs with choosing this path. It's not that you can't still participate in conferences or other training, but if you're forgoing those things for something that's more vigorous, mention it.

5. Financial structure and support requested

Now it's time to be clear with your investment request and outline what you want in terms of tuition-cost reimbursement, days covered, etc. Reiterate what the total cost of your program is, and ask for more than you might be comfortable asking for initially. If you ask for the very far end of the spectrum of what you could get, you will have room to negotiate. Aim high, and use your judgement as far as what's realistic in your organization, checking in on precedent and what's happening for your organization. Consider timing of when budgets are approved, if there have been layoffs, or what the profitability and sales trends are. Consider alignment to the annual development-planning process or performance-management cycle. Be situationally aware of the current mood of your organization and know your audience.

This section should also include how long you will stay with the company after your graduation, and the terms and conditions of repayment if you resign before you complete the length of time you've agreed to stay. Be specific to include dates and repayment schedules. Doing a combination of internal and external research on what's been done before is helpful to validate that what you're proposing matches the market.

When an employer is paying for the program, many MBA applicants ask for a maximum term of three years post-graduation employment, with a pro-rated repayment plan if the individual leaves the organization earlier (usually pro-rated in one-year terms). More frequently, however, we've noticed a shift in this expectation. Many employers are investing now with more trust (versus a contract) because they see the return right away. In today's job market, top talent is being placed readily and employers realize that a required retention term is not an effective incentive to keep an employee engaged over the long term.

Moreover, employers are recognizing that the ROI of an MBA is generally immediate as their candidate is applying the theories and tools learned and is forced to be more productive at work than previously due to new strains on their capacity. Finally, although an MBA is expensive, individuals are seeing the long-term strategic view of their careers more readily (long gone are the days of staying with one employer for the duration of your career) and are willing to make career moves to match. People are more willing to accept a payback scheme and then seek a signing bonus from a new employer to help compensate for any required payback to a previous employer.

As time-driven payback terms seem to be declining, asking for company focused projects and/or engagement measures (that allow you to use your MBA on the job, are aligned with your goals, and benefit the company) are rising in popularity and worth considering as an alternative payback measure.

Make note of how vacation and time spent in the classroom will be covered, and it's often helpful to offer to use some of your vacation to cover days needed for the classroom. Also note again if you are forgoing other conferences or training here.

As part of your terms and conditions, consider including an agreement with scheduled check-ins to a leader a level or two above you as a formal way for the business to stay connected with you and your learning throughout the process. (See Chapter 5 on formalizing this process with skip-level meetings we call "step-through meetings".) Not only does this hold you accountable, but it's a valuable opportunity to inform your business early and often.

6. Work management plan

While it might seem obvious that you don't want to fall short of your work commitments as you earn your MBA, it is worth stating this commitment in a logistics plan for your employer. This is your opportunity to clearly acknowledge and mitigate any concerns your employer may have about your current responsibilities being compromised throughout this undertaking. Assure your employer that you anticipate a heavy workload, but you have a plan to manage both school and work.

Your plan should be customized to your work role and the demands of your program. You might consider a calendar format outlining school days, when you're able to work longer days at work, and any key dates for your organization that you will prepare for (budget or performance review cycles, for example). Your plan should demonstrate thoughtful anticipation of the demands for your business and role, and how you'll adapt. If you have the kind of work that includes an on-call component, note how you'll prioritize a crisis event and that you're still available and ready for your core duties, or have a contingency in place for when you're unavailable.

Close this section and the business case by thanking your decision-maker for their consideration, and include a summary of next steps with actions and due dates. Offer to be available for any follow-up questions.

(Note: We've included this section assuming you're working full time. However, even if you're working part-time and don't think your work will be impacted, if you're asking for employer support of any capacity (say, even flexibility of schedule), it's worth demonstrating that you're thinking ahead to reduce the chance your duties will suffer during the program.

7. Appendix (optional)

Approach this section with caution, and only add items that reinforce something you've referenced in another section. This isn't about adding volume; it's about adding substance and further support for your case. You may include letters of reference and awards you've earned or provide details on how courses will apply to your current and future roles if you haven't done that in a previous section. This is also the spot to add news articles or academic papers about the value of an MBA, or news coverage of your chosen program and its graduates.

Action tip:
Make a list of your best successes and strengths

If the concept of selling yourself feels about as comfortable as snacking on glass, you're not alone, and it doesn't have to feel that way. Taking the time to self-reflect and advocate for yourself takes preparation and practice. Build your confidence by creating a list (just for you) of what you've accomplished and what that could look like in the future with advanced education. It's a list of why you're awesome – for real. No one can advocate for you like you can. Besides, how will anyone else know how to advocate for you if you don't frame what that advocacy could sound like?

To create your list of your best successes and strengths, focus on your strengths and skills, completing statements such as:

"Here are my main contributions..."

"I'm an exceptional leader because...

"My unique selling point or value proposition is that I..."

"I feel best when I'm working on..."

"I'm most proud of..."

We know this isn't easy. Articulating these answers becomes easier when you focus on your strengths with a regular practice that includes documenting your self-reflection, which becomes a muscle you build over time. And remember, you are super committed to being intentional with your MBA, and that is just the start of the success to come.

Pitching your case

Once your case is drafted, it's time to prepare for the submission process. Have some trusted people in your life review your draft and get their feedback. Let the person you're submitting to know about your case with a conversation ahead of formally submitting your business case. You want to introduce this idea in person, in a conversational setting. If that's not possible, introduce the idea during a phone call. As always, how this conversation looks will depend on who you're talking to and the culture of your workplace, but focus on planting the seed and positioning your interest in talking more with your decision-maker about this next step in your career. The goal is to avoid surprising your decision-maker with the business case. You've been working diligently on your case, and it's now time to start sharing your thoughts and journey with the people who will help make it all a reality.

Next, submit your business case electronically or in hard copy and schedule time to connect for follow up. Include a copy of your business case in the meeting request, and book this quickly. Work with administrative assistants ahead of time to ensure you can get the meeting time and explain why it can't be moved. You need this time and conveying a sense of urgency at the outset will keep your momentum going and allow you to meet your timelines.

When you're in person speaking to your business case, take the time to talk through the most important parts, highlight your strengths, and ask for questions. Don't do all the talking. A conversation has two people in it, so remember your audience and include them along the way. Wait about two weeks for a response and approval, and then follow up. Pay close attention to what's going on for your company and the decision-maker you're working with so that you can follow up in a way that's not too invasive and respects their time.

Whether you get approval or not, follow up with everyone who helped you prepare (those who shared information, booked a meeting, or offered proofreading, etc.) by taking the time to thank them. Like the practice of self-reflection, the practice of formally thanking people who support you puts your intention into action and demonstrates gracious leadership.

Renée's MBA business case experience:

At the start of my MBA journey, I hadn't met Christine, and I hadn't written this book, so I didn't yet realize my own business case generally followed this format. I worked in a casual environment and my own case to my vice-president and manager at the time was similarly informal, but I did begin by doing my research of MBA programs available locally and abroad, as well as lots of self-reflection on the kind of experience I wanted to have. I met with several colleagues who had done their MBAs while working full-time for our company and asked how they had managed and who had paid.

The norm in our organization was that little or no money was available for tuition, but that lots of consideration was given for time away from the office. I considered this carefully, and knew that culturally, getting tuition paid for was going to be beyond what someone in my role could reasonably expect. I built my case around asking for time off to attend regular and block-week courses and highlighted that I was contributing a hundred percent of the financial cost because I believed it was worth the investment and that my commitment to my daily duties would not suffer.

My leadership team quickly became my biggest advocates and supporters, and remain so to this day. One other advantage of self-financing is that you're a free agent after graduation, which I was sure to clarify in my business case; the support of the time off I was given didn't oblige me to an employment term outside of my existing contract.

Christine's MBA business case experience:

I followed the format outlined above, and it resulted in eighty-five percent compensation (including paid time-off for intensive weeks and half of the days for the international business trip), with a one-year retention term. The organization I worked with at the time, although 40,000 employees strong, had never paid for an employee's MBA before. The request was well outside of the scope of the tuition-reimbursement program. I knew I had to go to the top to have this investment even considered, let alone approved. I wrote the business case as described and positioned it first with my leader to gain support, buy-in, and effective championship. She made sure to allow her leader to provide feedback and help shape the proposal, and we finalized it together. This created a sense of ownership on behalf of my leader's leader, who then offered to position the request with the President and CEO in advance of me finding time with him to discuss. That leader knew the business case had to be exceptionally strong; so strong that she would get agreement to do something the company had never done before — invest in an employee's MBA. It was a remarkable success, and I ensured all program deliverables were done for the organization, thereby providing an immediate ROI, in addition to fulfilling the retention term.

Executive communication template

Preparing your case verbally is as important as preparing a great business-case document. Consider these communication preferences when preparing to deliver any case to executives and the highest levels of leadership. It's definitely OK to make notes in preparation. Always consider your audience and ask yourself what you can say to more effectively relate to them.

Through Christine's experience as a certified practitioner of many leadership- and communication-style psychometric assessments, and as an executive coach, she has observed four fundamental ways in which people prefer to receive and interpret information. Consider these in advance of a conversation to enhance the impact of your intended message.

Concrete

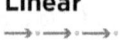

These individuals require facts that validate ideas, theories, practices, etc. They are always looking for evidence in data to find solutions to problems or challenges.

Linear

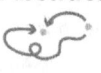

People who prefer to receive information in a linear way require sequencing and structure that is clear and easy to follow. Their thinking is linear in the way they take in information (step by step) and communicate it to others.

Abstract

These individuals require rationale and context to understand ideas and concepts being presented. They enjoy the big-picture perspective and the possibilities and connections that exist between thoughts.

Relationship

These individuals associate what they know personally to the idea being communicated. They enjoy feeling connected through personal experience and are more ready to engage and interpret when the relationship is clear.

To structure your communication effectively to appeal to all audiences, follow this conversation structure:

Begin
- Connect with your audience and introduce your topic *(relationship)*
- Succinctly summarize your main message or point *(abstract)*
- Review the objectives and agenda *(linear)*

Evolve
- Support your idea by providing data and information where possible to expand on the points made in the opening *(concrete)*

Conclude
- Restate your opening comments, review learning objectives *(abstract)*
- Deliver a call to action *(relationships)*
- Summarize action items and next steps *(linear)*

Conversation guidelines

Here's a framework for successfully preparing for and navigating the important conversations you face. This is for those times when you want to ask for more (salary, position, etc.), give tough feedback, have a group discussion to achieve a desired outcome, and/or prepare to coach an employee or peer, etc.

Really, this guide is for any important conversation that you want to make sure you prepare for to increase your probability of success. The stages of every conversation are highlighted and will prompt you to think about who you're speaking to and what matters most. You don't have to follow it verbatim, though you can have it handy as your guide. The focus here is on the preparation and planning to give you the confidence to speak authentically, offering value to what you're saying and being clear about the next steps in every conversation you have.

1. **Begin** | Identify the purpose of the meeting to clarify what you'd like to talk about. Be sure to share why it's important.

2. **Confirm** | Clearly communicate the situation, issue, concern, questions, or idea that you'd like to discuss during the meeting. Clarify the situation and what you believe to be true, and consider how you might adapt your messaging to the person you are communicating with based on their tendencies and preferences.

3. **Evolve** | Start the conversation and create the desired discussion. Be aware of going off topic and bring the discussion back to its purpose, if needed. Create an agenda for your meeting in advance and think through what you want to say at each stage of the discussion to help keep it on track and ensure you achieve the desired outcome.

4. **Acknowledge** | Review the discussion and commitments made and summarize the action items that have resulted from the meeting. What will look different as a result of the meeting? To prepare, consider what success looks like and what your desired outcome may be.

5. **Conclude** | Express appreciation, confirm final details, and re-emphasize any important points. It's best practice to reflect on all important conversations you have by asking yourself what you did well and what you could have done differently.

1. Begin   2. Confirm   3. Evolve   4. Acknowledge   5. Conclude

The right people in your corner: Build a powerful support network, get an executive coach

When a boxer steps into the ring, it might look like they're alone in facing an opponent, but they're not. They have a whole team in the background, in their corner, helping them to fight their best. They're not alone, and you shouldn't be either.

Pulling together a powerful support network is about knowing where you need help and enlisting the right help through genuine relationships that you maintain vigorously. Think of it as creating an intentional system designed to help you be at your best where you need it most. A support network can include any person or people providing you services. Some common examples are mechanics, stylists, therapists of all specialties, cleaners, meal providers, candid friends, people who remind you to have fun and take a breath, family, pets, etc.

Just like a solid school team can propel your MBA journey to higher success than you can achieve on your own, having a formidable team in your personal life is essential to doing your best work at school and beyond. As we like to say, there's extraordinary power in an intentionally built support network, and you need to get the right people in your corner.

Now, you may be thinking that you have all of these people in your life already, so how is thinking of them as a connected support network any different? It's different because of how you view a support network, and that view changes your actions and what you receive from the network in turn. When you're invested in an intentionally built support network, we believe that investment is felt and reciprocated by those included. The mindful way to build a network is through long-term thinking based on relationships and mutual benefit. You should always choose your network carefully, looking for like-minded providers and people who can support your short- and long-term needs.

Seeing yourself as supported by a team of profession-als and trusted people who help you to be your best self is mindfulness in action. Knowing you've got a dedicated team behind you will also help you feel less alone when the work is piling up. Knowing who to reach out to when you need help is invaluable.

Action tip:
Building your support network with intention

Use these questions to mindfully map your support network. The goal is to create a strong personal support group that you can rely on for mutual benefit. Draw or record who's in your personal support network in a journal or in a file on your desktop or tablet for easy reference.

- What are the areas in which I can use some professional or emotional support? (Think of this as who can help you devote the most of your time to your studies, team work, family life, and career aspirations.)

- When and how will I engage these professionals and trusted people for support? Book each of these appointments at the frequency that suits you a semester (or quarter, if you prefer) at a time. For trusted people, schedule in phone calls, text messages or group chats, visits, important celebrations, etc. Plan to connect so you don't forget.

- How can I show each of them my gratitude for their service and the role they play in supporting my success? This can be as simple as expressing it explicitly to them (simple, but something often forgotten) to referrals, gifts, or handwritten messages. Relationships are reciprocal, so be sure to let people know how important they are to your day-to-day success.

Note: Your personal support network should reflect your needs and your exacting standards. Don't be afraid to move on from a provider or personal relationship if the fit no longer works. Like any network, your personal support system is dynamic.

Hire an executive coach for an even better ROI

Many MBA programs offer a coaching service as part of the program. If yours does – excellent. Take full advantage of this service. If your program does not have a coaching service, start looking for a coach to help you navigate your experience and the development that goes along with it.

Coaching is the practice of helping people discover the possibilities they don't think exist for themselves. Good executive coaches can help people challenge the status quo, break through barriers and obstacles in the way of success, and explore the unknown through a series of practices, tools, and resources. Coaches are active listeners who ask insightful questions, exploring and challenging your development. The goal of coaching is to help you articulate your behaviours in a personal-development strategy (a plan that is unique to you), focusing on how you are perceived so that you can elevate your contributions.

This book is a great start to building the self-reflection and practices to help you get maximum ROI on your MBA. A dynamic relationship with a trained and certified coach can help you enhance your ROI even further in a personal, one-to-one way. We see a live coach as a powerful addition to the guide and foundation we provide here.

A coach can also work with you on specific leadership-development strategies. This is important because if there's a gap between the leadership development that your school offers and what you need and want, a coach will help you fill that skills gap with personal focus and accountability. After graduation, a professional and experienced coach can help you realize the return on investment from your MBA that you set out to get. They can help you make the best use of your MBA and career by being intentional and focused about what you want to create for yourself and the people you lead.

To find a coach near you, visit coachfederation.org and look for the coach-finder tab. As they state on their website, the International Coach Federation (ICF) is the leading global organization dedicated to advancing the coaching profession by setting high standards, providing independent certification, and building a worldwide network of trained coaching professionals.

Just like with an MBA program and the people you choose for your personal support network, a coach should be a good fit for you personally. Do your research and ask about their approach. Ask if the coach also has an MBA. The ability to understand and appreciate through personal experience what you are experiencing as an MBA student or graduate inevitably allows them to be better equipped as your coach. Consider asking coaches if they have a coach for themselves. Coaching is an art and an ongoing practice of improvement. The best coaches have their own coach because they're deeply committed to the process and benefits of coaching.

Why a coach is worth it

From the professional executive coach, Christine:

A lot of people assume the most important education through an MBA program is what you learn in the classroom and from the textbooks, essentially the curriculum and required content of the program. What I've seen in my years of working with MBAs across

North America during and after their studies, as well as with business professionals at all levels and stages in their careers, is that many clients are looking for ways to apply what they've learned formally on the job. What you've learned is one thing, but what you do with it to be a better leader, and better in business, is an entirely different thing.

The application of what you've learned formally is exactly what a professional coach is here to help you do. All of our clients at Bright Wire find great value in a coaching partnership because it's the one opportunity in their busy day where they can create space to talk about and reflect on developing themselves. That conversation is beyond who the client is and what they've done; it's about exploring the behaviours possible as a result of the client's knowledge gained in the MBA program, or their professional experiences in general. Ultimately, those behaviours drive better results for the client's business, career and personal satisfaction.

The other reality most leaders face is that they spend a lot of time developing others and providing constructive feedback to those around them, but not doing the same for themselves. Most organizations only have yearly opportunities to get feedback. That's not enough time to spend on your personal development.

What I enjoy the most about being an executive coach is helping people to accomplish new realities. I see them focus beyond their current reach and have the confidence to get there relatively simply. One client of mine, whom I'll call John, recently experienced this transformation. John had a long track record of success, yet felt there were simply no promotion opportunities available to him at his current company. Other than debating taking his MBA, he didn't (and couldn't) imagine what was next.

Through a trusting coaching partnership, I prompted John to set those current realities (or at least perceived realities) aside to create his ideal scenario for the work he most wanted to do. I then asked him what might be possible if he put his business-school skills to the test by creating a business case for the dream role he had just described. He created a business case for it and found that it made a lot of sense with great benefit to his company. At this point, I asked him what was stopping him from presenting this solid business case to his boss. He presented the case and got a promotion for a role that hadn't even existed until he created it. Afterwards, we reflected on what created that success with appreciation for the barriers John had overcome. We did this so that he could repeat it with specific and mindful behaviours in the future.

John's story is a great example of the value of taking time for yourself and focusing on your personal development, because no one is going to do this work for you but you. An executive coach is solely dedicated to you and your success. Our priority is supporting your best interests.

From the experience of being coached, Renée:

A coach fills a unique space in life. They are someone who is on your side but is also there to be impartial and honest at the same time. That's a beautiful combination where you will get targeted feedback designed to help you. If the best teams and athletes have coaches, why wouldn't I have the same for my development as a human and leader?

In my experience, each of the things I did with my coach was easy enough to do and yet had a major impact on my day-to-day experience. I was amazed at how one little exercise could start to create changes immediately with tangible results. I wouldn't think of incorporating a coach as adding something to an already crammed schedule; think of it as a small thing you can do to be incredibly more effective and efficient with your time.

More than anything, especially as someone who struggles to ask for help as much as I should, it's easy to choose to go it alone when things get hard. Reaching out means being vulnerable. Things are already tough, so why do one more thing that's so hard to do? And so many of us choose to be tough by going it alone. Or at least we try to look that way. But that's almost never the right answer to successfully accomplishing the hardest challenges. It's certainly not the way to get the most of the experience.

Having a coach meant that I had a system in place to get help on the most important aspects of my development before I fell into an old habit.

Action tip:
Make the business case for an executive coach after you graduate

Many employers will cover the cost of an executive coach. To convince yours, prepare a business case for the value this service will provide to the organization through your growth and improved performance. Follow our template on page 55, with special consideration to these key coaching objectives:

- Improve leadership and communication skills that will enhance your personal performance and that of your team

- Cultivate a more strategic view, challenge assumptions, shift perspectives, and achieve rapid personal development

- Combine personalized development and ongoing accountability so that knowledge translates into new behaviour

- Overcome challenges, implement changes, and facilitate learning that is most important to you and your organization

- Eliminate self-deception or blind spots (what an individual can't, won't, or doesn't see) and create accountability for improvement

Chapter 4
Purpose and presence: Maintaining mindfulness and intention throughout

The North Star – your GPS for the MBA journey ahead

Navigation systems are as old as people. We've always had a need for directions to where we need to go – a blueprint for the great unknown. Today, digital navigation systems are so ubiquitous we forget how central they are to helping us along our way. We'd be lost without them. As you consider the journey of an MBA, you will need some directions to help you along your way (and Google maps won't be able to help you here). You will always have the choice to get lost or to be on your path – the direction you take is truly yours.

Some of the oldest navigation systems are based on following the stars; this shining example can serve you in your life and particularly during your MBA journey. Each one of us has a built-in North Star that we calibrate toward to make sure we're headed in the right direction. Even if you haven't thought of it this way before, we think you'll find the concept true and useful.

As we move through life, growing into adults, navigating our careers, and making personal and recreational choices, there's always something, *that one thing* that has always guided us to make our decisions throughout our lives. Maybe the thing that has guided you is a word, phrase, theme, or feeling. It's a yearning. It occurs because you want to fulfill something based on your desire to contribute in this life, in this world. This one thing that repeatedly pulls you in a direction is your North Star, your internal global positioning system, which helps you find your place in the world.

If you decide to take an MBA, that unique journey is part of your path to constant fulfillment. Or, if you already have your MBA, you can still reflect and revisit your MBA journey and its value to you now. (Keep reading for Leena's reflection on her purpose after graduating with her MBA.) This yearning force, your North Star, is behind everything you do; examining what that is for you and where you are relative to it makes all the difference.

Now, we know that some of you may be discounting this as a concept that simply has no room in your fast-paced life or in your business. We've heard it before: "Don't spend my time up in the air. I want to be down here on earth getting stuff done." You've got an MBA to earn, after all. Here's the deal: If you don't look up and check in with your central purpose and the thing you care most about, or apply that purpose, you're wasting your time getting the wrong stuff done. Just like in navigation, your personal North Star guides you and keeps you on course. It's strategic and valuable to take time to both define your North Star and to check in on your progress to make sure you're getting the maximum fulfillment of any on-the-ground experience; MBAs and big business included.

Investing time to define your North Star also helps you to mitigate the challenges ahead and avoid regrets. If you're constantly asking whether the decision you're about to make helps you to achieve your North Star, you're well on your way to avoiding living your life as a box-ticking exercise and getting lost. In an MBA context, simply ticking that box is an expensive and inefficient undertaking. When things don't feel right in our lives, or we feel lost, it's because our actions haven't aligned with our North Stars.

Action tip:
Finding your North Star

The goal of this exercise is to understand what you're hoping for and to articulate it for yourself so you have a guiding principle to check back in on.

Finding your North Star takes some self-reflection. Claim some quiet time in your day for this activity, and have a conversation with yourself around these questions:

> *What themes are present as I look through my career and life?*

> *What kinds of education and experiences have I sought?*

> *What am I yearning for?*

> *What's most important to me?*

> *What's one way or standard I often use to measure my success?*

Look for recurring themes and think of a word or phrase that captures your strongest sentiment. Record your word or phrase on a sticky note and put it somewhere as a prompt to revisit it often.

Reconnecting with your North Star after graduation

Leena's post-MBA experience:

A whole year had passed since Leena graduated from her MBA program, and yet the promotion she craved had not yet materialized. She had always sought out challenges in her life and career, but was struggling to find traction. Leena was feeling lost. To reconnect with her purpose and help her articulate why she completed her MBA, she tried the North Star action tip. Here's what she recorded in her journal:

What themes are present as I look through my career and life?

I've always valued achievement and making progress. I'm obsessed with metrics! If I can measure something, I want to work to earn a high score. I have embraced challenges, especially when others won't. I like being in charge and having freedom in my work.

What kinds of education and experiences have I sought?

In my undergraduate years, I was president of my residence hall. I took on the most challenging internship assignments two summers in a row. My grades were top of my class. When I took on my MBA, I led a team to a business case competition, and we won first place. I also graduated at the top of my cohort and was on the honour roll.

What am I yearning for?

An executive-level position where I can directly influence the strategy of a large company. I want to win at the top levels of an organization. I'm looking for high compensation and public rewards from my work.

What's most important to me?

A sense of high achievement. Competition and winning. Being known for strong leadership.

What's one way or standard I often use to measure success?

Promotions and the status that comes with them.

Looking at her responses, Leena wondered what had happened to her competitive drive since she'd graduated her MBA. "It's pretty clear that my North Star shines around competing and winning, and that I look for that consistently," she reflected. "And yet, I feel like I've been waiting for someone to issue the competition terms. I've always gone after what I wanted and didn't wait for anyone else to lay out the rules of the game." Leena then focused her reflection on what had been holding her back. She realized that she had not taken a proper rest after completing her MBA and decided that some focused quiet time would be helpful to her in realigning her current behaviour with what she truly wanted. It was time to reignite her competitive nature to achieve her c-suite aspirations.

When you're following your North Star, you can't get lost

"When you find your North Star, you know where you're headed. That alone feels good," says Dr. Rick Hanson, psychologist and senior fellow of the Greater Good Science Center at UC Berkeley.[6] "Plus, your North Star is (presumably) wholesome and vital, so aiming toward it will bring more and more happiness and benefit to yourself and others. And you can dream bigger dreams and take more chances in life, since if you lose your way, you've got a beacon to home in on."

As you consider your MBA journey, dedicate time to putting a plan together for how you will ensure you aim for your North Star throughout your MBA experience and what specific steps you will take to accomplish that. Working full time and earning your MBA is going to be the equivalent of steering a ship in rough seas. Plan now for those storms so you can navigate the rough waters expertly.

Christine's North Star and her MBA experience:

My North Star is about being my best self, which is found by seeking continual learning and that next level of understanding and awareness. The MBA program was an enabler of attaining my North Star.

How this showed up for me in my MBA was by my focusing more on subjects like finance and data modelling, rather than human resources and economics, which were the subjects I was more comfortable in. I thought that if I was there to learn as much as I could, I was going to play more in the finance and

....

6   Hanson, Rick. "Just One Thing: Find Your North Star." Greater Good Magazine, May 11, 2012. https://greatergood.berkeley.edu/article/item/just_one_thing_find_your_north_star.

data-modelling space – the subjects I wasn't familiar with. When things become so busy and you're trying to balance the demands of the program and life, it gets difficult to keep leaning into subjects that are not the most efficient. It's always easy to do what you know, but I kept at it and continually asked for more challenges. I learnt a lot!

My North Star comes from being from a family where education was a matter of when, not if. My parents were constantly learning, growing, taking courses, and asking bigger questions. They are really curious people and advocates for education. Now, I'm able to serve my North Star by helping my clients find theirs.

Renée's North Star and her MBA experience:

I yearn for adventure. That singular word is my measuring stick for everything I set out to do. Others may look at my life or choices and not think they're very adventurous picks at all, but adventure is all relative. A North Star is a deeply inward and personal concept, and I'm the only one who has to know something was an adventure. I know I'm on an adventure when I'm taking some risks, getting uncomfortable, and testing my resilience. I'm solving problems and exploring myself and other people, and my actions are powered by curiosity and a desire for deeper learning. When I look back on my life, seeking adventure is the recurring theme. I find a lot of joy and humour in the adventures I've taken.

Every day was an adventure during my MBA, and I was focused on getting the most out of each moment. I was very focused on the experience, and embraced being uncomfortable and the challenges of not knowing what would be most valuable. That perspective made the challenges enjoyable. I also think adventures are best shared, so I made sure I connected with the adventurous *experiences of my classmates because understanding their experience enhanced mine.*

In collaborating on this book, we discovered that our North Stars have a lot in common around learning and curiosity. Finding your own North Star also helps you to find people on similar paths, and that's where some incredible business opportunities can be born. The more we are clear with regard to our direction, the easier it is to find others to achieve great journeys with.

Never stop looking up as you create your blueprint for your journey to the great unknown.

Showing up on the playground

As you start your chosen MBA program, consider being intentional about the way you show up. Though the setting is more grownup and professional, you're the new kid at the playground, and you've got some choices to make. No one knows you (probably), everyone is new (most often), and this is your chance to start from scratch on who you want to be at this playground. You can develop new skills and try things in a low-risk way because you're building networks and relationships where no one has a preconceived notion of who you are.

Often, people won't try new things around those they know because they don't want to be perceived as inauthentic, or because they operate with a fear of failure and a fear of disappointing someone. With a new program and new people, however, you get an opportunity to try some things on without the worry of familiar expectations to stand in your way. The risk of disappointment is little to none. We're not encouraging you to be inauthentic (please always keep it real); rather, we encourage you to shed some of the perceptions you may have of your abilities (or inabilities) as you begin the MBA journey. This is the time to cultivate a mindset that allows you to have the confidence and courage to try new things. Your program is a development opportunity to explore safely.

Be curious about the secondary learning available to you outside of the curriculum. Being surrounded by this many ambitious, committed, highly competent, smart, and interesting people is a rare opportunity in life. Take a moment to realize you can learn from this fascinating environment, finding development through the experience, group and personal dynamic, diverse demographic, and the people and leadership experience that comes with the classroom. You must be aware of this opportunity to learn and grow from it, so the first step starts with giving yourself permission to try new things and to see the development opportunities that are all around you.

When you start your MBA program, get to know who's in your class as soon as possible. A class list is usually provided ahead of time, and that's your cue to start researching and planning who you'll connect with. Think about your future and what lies ahead for you as far as industries and companies. Revisit your career-path assessment regularly as a reminder of with whom you may want to prioritize building a relationship. It will be important to connect on a personal level, and as you connect, remember to think beyond some of the personal attributes you may have in common to opportunities to collaborate, learn new things together, or try new skills.

Beware of falling into cliques and hanging out with the same people all of the time. Go out of your way to hang out with different people. Consider that your classmates are experienced professionals likely to have large networks. Even a quick search of your classmates' LinkedIn profiles will likely show that each person you meet potentially opens your network by another 500 to 1,000 people. The ratio of the value of expanding your network to the time it takes to do it is quite high, so be deliberate by sitting and talking with one new person each time your classes are in session.

Your brand

You are leaving an impression from the moment you apply, to the moment you graduate, and in all the moments well beyond. As you go through your MBA experience with intention, your personal brand is something to be aware of always. A personal brand is much like the commercial brands we're familiar with in the products and services we buy. A strong brand is easily recognizable, consistent, and tells customers what they can expect from choosing that product. Your personal brand works the same way; it helps to establish who you are quickly so that your customers (people you want to build relationships with) can choose you.

Your personal brand is much more than what you wear or your grooming and general appearance, although those things are, of course, important. Your personal brand is your relationships, how you advocate for what's right and wrong, the questions you ask, what you're known for, how you engage others in the learning experience, etc. These are all things to be aware of, and with habit, paying attention to them can become part of a secondary degree of consciousness throughout your MBA experience.

Because MBA students go through such intense experiences together, often through intensive course weeks and group work, you build trust with your classmates quickly and that allows you to let your guard down quickly, too. Go with this, even if it feels uncomfortable at first. Use the chance to open and develop your relationship-building skills. During each interaction, deal with each person as though they could be your future employer, employee or partner. You can still have a lot of fun, but consider your personal brand in the context of earning your MBA and what's beyond graduation. Don't under-estimate the potential future risks of being complacent about relationship and personal-brand building today.

When Christine was halfway through her MBA program, she noticed the dress code was starting to slip, particularly on Saturdays. She rallied a few individuals, who softly campaigned to put the business back into business school by focusing on what they wore, even on Saturdays. In this Executive MBA program, class was held on Fridays and Saturdays, and the tendency over time, especially as assignments piled up and students got tired, was to start dressing down on Saturdays. The group of students who committed to staying in business clothes had the strongest network afterward because they were always viewed as being professional. How we look and feel affects how we act. That kind of an impression leads to lots of other opportunities to connect and learn on a deeper level.

As the saying goes, don't dress for the job you have (which in this case could be an exhausted student working on a Saturday), dress for the job you want (the career of your dreams) by putting your personal brand into action. Let's get beyond the clothes to get your brand truly dressed for the career of your dreams.

Developing your personal brand

Elements of a personal brand

A personal brand is the total experience someone has with who you are and what you represent as an individual and as a leader.

People with strong brands are clear about who they are. They know and maximize their strengths.

Your personal brand is what you stand for - the package of character traits and capabilities that make who you are, expressed in a way that others understand right away.

Less than five percent of people are living their personal brands consistently. However, seventy percent of professionals believe they have defined their personal brands and fifty percent believe they are living them. This is often where a person has placed focus on self-promotion rather than a commitment to advance themselves by serving others[8].

Less than fifteen percent of people have truly defined their personal brands[7].

Why a personal brand matters

Others experience you as a package of traits and capabilities

Impressions are formed subconsciously - it's human nature.

Your reputation is how others see you.

If your reputation doesn't reflect your true brand, you'll miss opportunities.

People act based on those perceptions.

Balance

Don't be lulled into a false sense of an established reputation, saying things like, "I'm known as a high-potential person."

Corporate settings can make you unworried about building your personal brand, and that's a career mistake.

Two aspects of branding happen simultaneously between where you work and who you are - where does one end and the other begin?

. . . .

7   Llopis, Glenn, "Personal Branding is a Leadership Requirement not a Self Promotion Campaign," Forbes, April 8 2013, https://www.forbes.com/sites/glennllopis/2013/04/08/personal-branding-is-a-leadership-requirement-not-a-self-promotion-campaign/

8   Ibid

Personal brand is not the same as corporate brand

Your personal brand must resonate with you, and it needs to be different than the brand of the company you work for. Your personal brand can be (and often will be) complementary to the corporate brand you work within, but your personal brand should be distinct. You may put your career needs behind those of your client or employer, or you may not enjoy "playing politics" or "selling yourself". But that's the **wrong** way of thinking. If you want to succeed past the mid-level of an organization, you need a strong personal brand; one that you've made friends with and are comfortable finding graceful ways to let others know about. A strong personal brand acts as a foundation for a long and rewarding career.

Action tip:
Create your personal brand

Complete your personal brand elements

1. When describing yourself, write down words or phrases that come to mind for each element. Be as specific as possible in each area.

Values (what's most important in your life)

_____

_____

_____

Drivers (what motivates you)

_____

_____

_____

Reputation (what you're known for)

_____

_____

_____

Behaviours (what others see you do)

_____

_____

_____

Skills (what you're best at doing)

_____

_____

_____

Image (how you're seen by others)

_____

_____

_____

2. Identify the themes and translate them into personal brand statements:

I stand for...

_____

_____

_____

I am known for...

_____

_____

_____

I want to be known for...

_____

_____

_____

Reflected best self

Here's an optional exercise if additional feedback is desired to help build your brand.[9]

1. Identify respondents and ask for feedback on a specific time when you were at your best. You can use email, one-to-one conversations, or an online survey to get this information.

2. Recognize patterns.

3. Compose a summary.
   Check: Is this how you want to be perceived?
   Does this align with your personal brand?

4. Apply what you've learned to your job and personal brand.

....
9   Roberts, Laura Morgan, et al. "How to Play to Your Strengths." _Harvard Business Review_, January 2005.

What the word thinks of me

Evaluate your intentions **with** your **brand elements** and what you learned from **the feedback you received.** Your brand should be the accurate picture of you that you want to project. How does it compare to your reputation (how others perceive you)? Is there a gap between the two?

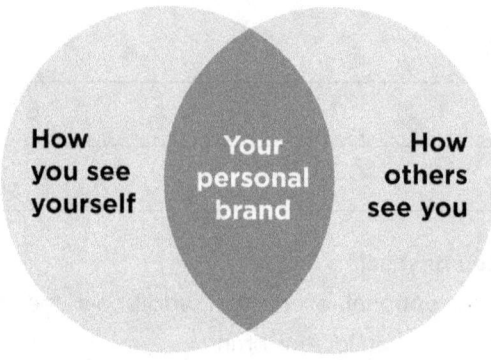

Defining the gap

Step one: research

- What is the total experience of having a relationship with you like?

  - Write down the top five things you would expect others to experience.

  - Have someone close to you do the same.

Step two: assess

- Are the answers the same or similar in meaning?

  - If yes – good for you.

  - If not – you have work to do.

Strategies to articulate your personal brand

- ☐ Find an internal career sponsor/brand advocate. This is someone who will share your personal marketing message, much as someone who loves a product will tell others about why the product is so great.

- ☐ Create a virtuous cycle that builds greater confidence. Momentum is important when advertising yourself, so start with one small thing that builds to the next, which will boost your confidence and keep you going. You don't have to do all of this in one day, just get the cycle rolling.

- ☐ Establish three marketing channels to share your brand: verbal, physical, written.

- ☐ Nail your instant credibility statement every time. A credibility statement is a simple, succinct, and memorable way to introduce yourself. See more on creating yours on page 151.

- ☐ Develop your managerial courage for presenting with impact. Practice always makes for better performance.

- ☐ Make use of stereotypes. Lean into the assumptions that may work for you and identify those that work against you.

- ☐ Be a person, not a label. Speak your mind and don't be a parrot (this is part of managerial courage).

- ☐ Leverage your points of difference. Highlight where you add value in ways that others cannot and find opportunities to use this.

- ☐ Invite others to see you in action. How can others know you have developed new skills if you don't provide them with opportunities to see you in action?

- ☐ Keep showing up. Be present both physically (in terms of how you use your posture and your body language) and mentally, by being confident and mindful of the way you contribute to the discussion, etc.

- ☐ Say it and you'll mean it. Share your personal brand with others. Use the words to describe how you want to come across. Not only will doing so influence others and have them more readily see you that way, it will be self-fulfilling where you will start to really represent your new brand in all of your interactions easily and authentically.

- ☐ Develop a narrative – a coherent story on how your past fits into the present. This is imperative to have, and it should not be thirty minutes long. Practice with three to five minutes as a starting point.

- ☐ Reintroduce yourself and re-educate acquaintances about your latest goals. Your leader may not know what you are learning in your MBA, or your network might not know about the most successful transformation project you just ran.

- ☐ Reassess regularly and re-invent if needed.

Managerial courage, as defined in Lominger's For Your Improvement[10]: Tactfully dispenses direct and actionable feedback; is open and direct with others without being

10   Lombardo, Michael M, and Robert W Eichinger. *FYI: For Your Improvement.* Lominger International, 1996.

intimidating; deals head-on with people problems and prickly situations.

Behavioral indicators:

- Achieving results in a manner that is consistent with organizational expectations
- Provides corrective feedback to others
- Deals with people problems and situations head-on
- Swiftly administers action (negative or positive) if a situation merits it

Here are examples from each of our intentional MBA guides and how they applied the branding work above to their personal situations. Your branding work may be more detailed than what's here for our three example MBAs, but this will give you a starting point to begin your own reflective process. The goal is to clarify your intentions and actions around how you share the story of who you are and where you're going.

This is also an important point to check in with your instant credibility statement (in Chapter 6) and make any updates based on your reflections of your personal brand. Remember that your instant credibility statement is an evolving way to tell your story. The skills you highlight about yourself create the perception and lasting impression you want.

You have a choice to tell your story the way you want it to be perceived. Avoid creating a narrow view by talking not about your expertise, but rather your transferrable skills. If you want to take on new projects in your current role, or highlight expanded capabilities, try to reshape what you highlight about yourself, while always being truthful.

Pre-MBA – Jessica's personal brand element example:

Steps 1 and 2:

> *Values:* challenge, fairness, meaningful work, growth, creativity

> *Drivers:* accomplishment, winning, creation, legacy, doing things successfully when people say I can't, freedom

> *Reputation:* hard working, dedicated, trusted, creative, reliable, ambitious, good listener, works too much, innovative, people want to work with me

> *Behaviours:* diligent, calm, and have an energetic side, active schedule, dedicated, casual

> *Skills:* listening, creating, design, storytelling, risk taking, process development, app design and maintenance, trend spotting, analytics, audience-focused design

> *Image:* Always with a laptop and sketch book; jeans and tops made by local designers; collector of sneakers and backpacks

Step 3:

- *I stand for… rewarding creativity, having freedom in my work, competing fairly, filling my days with activity and accomplishment.*
- *I am known for… being a good listener, having creative ideas, creating well-documented processes, showing dedication to projects and clients, taking creative and design risks, working hard, showing up on time, working too late.*

- *I want to be known for… having a strong business acumen, being a successful entrepreneur, creating apps that stand out from the rest, being a trusted partner with my clients.*

Some themes that stood out to Jessica in her brand were creativity, dedication, process, and trusted relationships. These will form the basis for her articulation and promotion of her personal brand.

"The top five things I would expect others to experience about me are: reliability, produces creative work, is a trusted listener, follows a clear plan and process, and works independently," says Jessica. She asked a close friend who she has also worked with to share her thoughts.

"With Jessica, I know she will always meet deadlines and leave a solid document of how she got the work done, so we can follow up. She has great ideas and will work really late to ensure they get done. Sometimes she focuses too much on work. I know she's really fun, but sometimes it's just hard to catch time with her. She takes on a lot," says Jessica's colleague and friend.

With this feedback, Jessica notices a disconnect where she sees herself as a trusted and skilled listener, but understands that others may find it hard to catch her attention due to her tendency to take on a lot of activities and projects. As Jessica develops her brand and her awareness of how she shares that brand, it's important for her to consider the feedback she's been given. Because Jessica values being a good listener, paying attention to her personal schedule and its impact on her ability to demonstrate she's truly listening will help her to maintain her intention and be authentic.

To create a virtuous cycle for sharing her brand and building her confidence, Jessica joins her local chamber of commerce's entrepreneurs' group. She commits to herself to attend a networking event with the group each month. This will give her a set time to practice her instant credibility statement and brand narrative.

Jessica also chooses a trusted colleague from the entrepreneurs' group to share her goals with. They talk about Jessica's upcoming MBA journey and how Jessica wants to be seen. Jessica asks this colleague for her help to spread the word about how Jessica is building her business acumen by going back to do her MBA to further grow her business and continue making the best apps for fellow entrepreneurs.

To further share the work she aims to do, Jessica plans to grow her reputation as a thought leader in app design by signing up for speaking engagements at two upcoming conferences. Jessica will also practice sharing her brand and telling her story in person at the chamber's entrepreneurial events each month.

Reflecting on her physical brand channels, Jessica knows it's important to be authentic. She also knows that her personal uniform of creative tops and sneakers might not help her build credibility as she works to establish herself beyond the clients she's currently working with. Jessica spends a lot of time considering how she shows up, and decides that she must focus on being consistent and authentic, while keeping the unique things about her that make her who she is. She is a creative person and wants to look the part, while being professional. She keeps her locally made, fun tops, as well as the sneakers, but adds a layer of intention with the accessories she chooses to make sure that she's polished and professional. Her laptop bag gets an upgrade, as do some of her sneaker choices. Her goal is to make each of her interactions consistent and professional.

Because she has her own website to promote her app business, Jessica updates her bio to be more focused on her improved brand articulation.

Jessica uses her monthly networking events to make sure she practices her new way of introducing herself. Additionally, she decides to dedicate just fifteen minutes each week to reflect on the ways she's articulated her brand that week, noting who she was able to share her message with and what the upcoming opportunities to share are.

Because Jessica currently leads a team at her corporate job, she has daily opportunities to flex her managerial courage. To punctuate her intention, she records in a journal at the end of each week how she did in each area of managerial courage. Working on this will help build her confidence to eventually leave her corporate role and become the entrepreneur she wants to be. She's also entering her MBA program with great intention and a fresh focus on how she shows up.

Mohammed's personal
brand element example:

Steps 1 and 2:

Values: family, education, career

Drivers: salary increase, more time with family

Reputation: technical expert who can be counted on,
dependable, friendly, and reserved

Behaviors: introverted style, formal, structured, methodical, analytical

Skills: technical expertise, analytical capability, analysis,
concept design, project management, strategic thinking,
cross-functional leadership, stakeholder engagement

Image: shy, reserved, steadfast in his commitment to
great work quality, usually wears khakis and button-up
shirts, serious

Step 3:

- *I stand for… doing the best at my work and being loyal to
  my family and employer.*
- *I am known for… always being counted on to deliver. I
  am deeply committed to the team and a valued technical contributor.*
- *I want to be known for… my broad skills outside of my
  technical expertise, which enable me to be successful.
  I enjoy leading and being in charge, and want to be
  recognized for modelling excellent leadership behaviours.*

Mohammed knows that the biggest gap he faces is that he's mainly seen for technical expertise and not as the leader he knows he is. Mohammed's focus needs to be on being intentional and targeted in his efforts to change his story.

"I know I need to go back to my instant credibility statement and make some updates, and that I need to practice it. A lot," says Mohammed. "I find this truly painful, so my challenge is going to be applying the discipline I have as an engineer to scheduling time to evaluate my statement and put it in action."

Mohammed's comfort zone is in an introduction like this: "I'm a pipeline-process lead engineer who has worked with pipeline companies for fifteen years." However, to tap into the magic of an updated instant credibility statement, Mohammed decides to go with this: "I'm an experienced leader in the energy sector, who has had success in running projects, overseeing budgets, and leading technical teams."

To hold himself accountable to staying outside his comfort zone and practicing his new introduction, he and an MBA classmate partner up to attend an upcoming leadership series happening near their offices. The series features brief chats and sit-down lunches, so Mohammed feels like that would be a comfortable environment for him to start one-on-one conversations with new people.

"The point about inviting others to see me in action is one that resonates with me," Mohammed says. "Given that I tend to be more on the quiet side of things, I know I need to be intentional about making sure I talk about the changes

I'm making in how I see myself and my personal growth as a leader." Mohammed decides that he needs to revisit the idea of the step-through meeting and connect with a leader he respects at his company. By committing to these meetings, Mohammed will have the chance to talk about what he's doing in his MBA program. He will focus his updates on how he's making sure he isn't just doing the kinds of things he knows he can excel at and that he's stretching himself and positioning himself as a leader.

For the visual aspect of this brand, Mohammed decides that he's pretty comfortable in his button-up shirts and khakis. However, he asks his wife to help him incorporate some more patterns and colors to help him visually stand out for when he chooses to be quieter vocally.

Leena's personal brand element example:

Steps 1 and 2:

Values: status, professionalism, determination, hard-work ethic, recognition, rewards, leadership

Drivers: making an impact, authority, autonomy, achievement, compensation

Reputation: as a valuable contributor, but have lost being an active part of the leadership conversation at my organization. My reputation has been established, and I feel like I've faded from the executive team's top of mind because I've been complacent in my position. I am not readily thought of for the next position, despite being known as reliable, stable, and experienced.

Behaviours: *serious, professional, politically savvy, tenacious, but also having a lack of initiative in some areas, perceived lack of confidence, struggle with promoting myself. I fundamentally believe that great work will just get noticed, and I feel like I should just keep my head down and do the work. I don't want to advocate for myself in a way that could be seen as too boastful and/or as bragging. I wasn't raised that way, and I'm not comfortable promoting myself.*

Skills: *action oriented, leadership, attention to detail, relationship building, strategy*

Image: *professional, active, serious*

Step 3:

- *I stand for… high-quality work, integrity, efficiency, driving for results and leading others.*
- *I am known for… all of the things above.*
- *I want to be known for… being a more strategic leader, capable of leading any function despite not having the technical expertise or direct experience. I want to be known for my ability to get results through people, and to be a macro-level leader who considers the holistic view and makes an impact on the total organization.*

Leena's company paid for her MBA, which she is grateful for, but she feels that she is now seen as having been totally taken care of as far as career development. There are development conversations happening of which she's just not a part. "*I feel like the company thinks I'll stick with them no matter what, and that my promotion opportunities are limited,*" *says Leena, who does have a contract to stay with the company for two years after graduation as part of her MBA financing. However, it's important to note that these kinds of contracts can usually be paid out if broken early. In Leena's case, it's clear that she needs to network beyond her company and look at other opportunities. Part of that process is opening herself up to ways she can be released from her contract rather than limiting herself. For example, a signing bonus at a new company can cover the cost of leaving a firm early. In any case, Leena needs to intentionally start to create opportunities in a place where she currently believes there are limited opportunities.*

Because Leena isn't seen the way she wants to be, her challenge is to build a new reputation. This process will start with refreshing her instant credibility statement and working to make that story known outside of her company (though she should still focus on sharing that story inside her company, too). For Leena, being intentional after graduation looks like a shift in how she talks about and positions herself in every interaction as the starting point for her to live into her new brand.

"I honestly feel a bit resentful about being sponsored to do my MBA and that nothing has happened since," says Leena. "At the same time, I know that I have to do the work to ask for what I want. Maybe the stories I've been telling myself about what's happening around my lack of promotion aren't exactly fact."

Leena has been experiencing some self-limiting beliefs and has stopped focusing on what's possible, dwelling instead on what's not happening. This is very common, and it's totally recoverable. It's a good reminder for everyone to not hold assumptions from the past as true and be really open to the possibilities of what can be available in the future. All that can be new is Leena's opportunity.

Leena revisits her career path (see her example on page 33) as a plan for where she will direct her efforts. To put her plan in motion, she begins by looking for strategic networks on LinkedIn so that she can engage with like-minded professionals outside of her current company. The opportunities to connect through a platform like this are almost limitless. We firmly believe that the effort Leena puts into participating in groups like this will be more than returned to her. Her goal will be to make connections on and offline.

Like Mohammed, Leena needs to revisit her step-through meetings (see page 134) and establish a new meeting series. Just because she's done her MBA doesn't mean she can't replicate this concept. Her focus for the step-through meetings will be on deliberate asks for what she wants as far as career advancement and will be supported by her new instant credibility statement that focuses on her transferrable skills and broad leadership potential. She will talk about her career path, being more vocal about what she truly wants to contribute and achieve as a leader with highly valuable transferrable skills.

As Leena moves ahead with her plans to expand her network, make her career aspirations better known in her organization, and explore opportunities beyond her current role, her confidence (both as it's perceived by others and felt by her) will grow. It's quite normal to feel less than confident as Leena did when she was expecting a lot of things to happen automatically after graduation. When things don't quite happen that way, it can feel like a blow and take some time to get back on course.

Chapter 5
Learning: Going beyond the curriculum

When we talk to MBA graduates about their regrets, many of them refer to things that relate to not taking relationships and their personal brands intentionally and seriously. We hear things like: I wish I hadn't complained so much about my employer, come across as so desperate about finding a new job, been so casual in language, appearance, and approach, not talked to new people or made more connections, etc. After graduation, many MBAs find the majority of what they've learned is a result of the secondary lessons outside of the course content and theory. As such, combining an intentional approach to how you show up and what you can learn from your environment is a wise use of your time. In this chapter, we'll explore some key areas beyond your program's curriculum that will allow you to show up as your best self, connect better with others, and learn more from the MBA environment.

Focus on having conversations with the people in your class right away, talking about who you are and what you're here to learn. Get to know people, and hear who they are and what they're there to learn. Remember your North Star? Keep in mind that your North Star is not the only star in this constellation, and how you work with other people's North Stars matters. Give others room to follow their lives' purposes. In business and in life, you're here to navigate different personality types, and your MBA experience is an opportunity to practice this route finding with grace. There's enough success for everyone – it's not a matter of one person winning over another. Working together to create safe learning and growing space for everyone simply creates more for everyone.

Reflection and feedback are critical to your development. Create a peer network to give you feedback when you're trying new things. (This can be part of your support network). Look to your classmates to set up a learning partner with which to exchange regular feedback.

Action tip:
Begin a learning journal

Behaviour changes are possible when you have an increased level of self-awareness and build your habits based on your progress. To build the habit of challenging yourself on a regular basis to learn outside of the MBA curriculum, create a calendar on your desktop or in your favourite app or journal. Then record there what new or different things you did each week and what you learned from them. Keep this file/app/book open always, so you can add to it easily as you experience networking and learning opportunities. Anything that causes you to pause and say to yourself, "Oh, interesting," should go in your learning journal.

Consider asking yourself these questions, or variations as needed, for each item you record:

How did it go?

What worked?

What did I learn?

What didn't work?

What am I most proud of?

What did I take away from the last class session that was a lesson outside of the course material?

How did others in my class come across?

How do my classmates build relationships?

How am I and others resolving conflict? What's working well here? What's not working?

Team charters,
a blueprint for working together

If you want to go fast, go alone.
If you want to go far, go together.
African proverb

Since most MBA programs are heavily focused on working in teams, it's wise to set the context for success from the start by building a team charter. Working in teams can be a valuable, rewarding, and exciting experience. We build bonds, get more things accomplished than anyone could alone, and celebrate winning together. But if a team is not aligned, teamwork can also be an awful experience where the group is focused on the wrong objectives, performing duplicate work, pulling late nights, and feeling awkward moments of tension and sometimes even head-on conflict between members. Having a team charter in place before you think you need one will save you time, allow you to better connect with each other, and effectively solve problems when they happen.

Many programs have students rotate through new teams each semester, or even by course. Depending on the program, teams may even be composed specifically to ensure students are exposed to people they wouldn't usually work with, encouraging/forcing students to get uncomfortable and stretch their working styles. It can feel at times as though you're in a petri dish of an experiment destined for friction and eventual combustion.

MBA programs *are* running a science experiment of sorts by making students work in teams because the nature of work and life is that we will have to learn to work with others effectively. We like to think we have a choice of who we work with in the real world, but most of the time, we don't. Whether it's an inherited team you're tasked with leading, a high-worth client with peculiar demands, or an organizational structure change you didn't see coming, you will always have to work with people who are different from you and whom you didn't choose.

Forced teamwork is not an evil experiment, and it doesn't have to be destined for a messy lab explosion either. Done right, teamwork fosters better results through stronger communication and builds real relationships where there's an increased respect for one another. In an MBA program, remember that your teams are part of your network – the people who will be your future bosses, collaborators, partners, colleagues, or even your next job opportunity.

You're building skills you can bring to the workplace as a leader where you're thinking of team dynamics and planning for high-performance results.

This takes time and commitment. And it starts with a great team charter.

Building your charter (yes, you really need one)

Most MBA programs start with some human resources and leadership-based courses to set up student teams for success. Intensive weeks/courses are popular beginnings to programs, where teams are focused on a specific task and work quickly in close quarters to accomplish new challenges.

In this concentrated and rigorous environment (they're called intensive weeks for valid reasons), students have no time to fumble with roles and responsibilities along the way; you're moving at such a quick pace that the bonding and performing elements of working together as a team are accelerated. Even if teams accomplish only half of what they set out to do in an intensive week, they have a feeling of accomplishment that is so high that some people end up believing this is the only team for them.

Reality check: You're getting a new team. Enjoy your intensive week, but don't be lulled by it if the team-bonding experience is positive. Your next team might connect well instantly, and you'll work together like magic with little effort. Or you won't. The scope and volume of deliverables increases dramatically after introductory intensive weeks, and students are challenged to contribute in new ways, often in ways that make them feel uncomfortable.

To mitigate teamwork problems, don't wait for a leadership opportunity to come to you or for the problems to start. Create a leadership opportunity by leading a team-charter conversation with your team. This can be as formal or informal as you choose, but we recommend you document your conversation in some way, ensuring that everyone has a chance to contribute and signs or acknowledges the agreement.

Team charter components

1. Team ambitions

Just like a company would, your team needs to set out the objectives they have been formed to achieve, what success will look like, and what's important to them along the way. Be clear on what your objectives are, on key milestones in the semester, and on what the course work will honestly look like when it comes down to doing it. Take the syllabus and examine it closely to plan appropriately for reading time, presentation preparation, group assignments, and learning new skills. Talk about grades – are they important or not? What's important to each team member, and how will the group represent that in their work? The more clearly you can map out a team approach that plans for and anticipates challenges, the more successful you will be.

2. Meetings, processes, and roles

This section should include the process and purpose of meetings and each person's duties and skills within the team.

Will your meetings have an agenda? Will action items be tracked and by whom? Is there a timekeeper? Are meetings chaired by a leader/facilitator? How late or early will the group go, and who/what decides? Will each person bring their own dinner or is that a rotating group responsibility? (This may sound like a trivial thing to discuss, but you need fuel to perform. Consider that you're also building a team culture, and that rituals are an important part of the bonding experience.) Where are documents stored and shared? Do all meetings happen in person? What does online/electronic collaboration and connection look like for your team? Get real about how you'll work together and coordinate.

Have each person share what their strengths are as well as their unique value proposition. What do they bring to the team? What do they need from the team? Is your group building and strengthening areas you're already good at or improving areas and skillsets that are new or challenging? What's each person's work style? What does each member need to learn?

3. Accountability and dispute resolution

How will your team give feedback on both behaviour and project work? What will you do to hold each other accountable to meet timelines and tasks? What will your team do when people do not deliver on their commitments? How will you resolve disagreements as a team? How will you connect with your professors and the university if there is a formal complaint, and at what stage would this happen? Setting out the process to deal with difficult things before they happen reduces the anxiety of resolving a conflict when it arises and saves time so that everyone can get back to the objectives and course work at hand.

4. Celebration and customs

Don't forget to mark your team's incredible achievements by planning to celebrate them. This doesn't have to be complicated. Maybe it's an end-of-semester potluck with families, a round of beers at the campus pub after a project is handed in, a weekly team workout, a movie night, or a lunch downtown once a month to just visit and connect. Having fun together is important for team bonding and managing stress.

Plan a team-building event – try something new together. Look for ways to connect in the work you do together. Even the smallest traditions your team shares can grow to be significant memories of your time together. This experience goes by quickly, so plan to have fun to make sure you do.

Keep it fresh

Your charter is only as good as the team's commitment to following it. Revisit your team's charter regularly to keep it alive;

at least check in mid-semester/project to reflect on the experience objectively, assess your team's progress, and make any changes needed.

Mohammed's team charter

As part of his ongoing work to develop his leadership skills, Mohammed led one of his semester groups to create this team charter. He worked with the group to get everyone's input and commitment and made sure to revisit their progress and accountability to their charter throughout the semester.

1. ***Team ambitions:*** *Our group will complete all assignments on time and in an organized approach, earning high grades. (B is the lowest we will accept.)*

   We will be a coordinated team that shares responsibilities and is seen as model of professionalism in the classroom.

   We value high standards, collaboration, process, and efficiency.

2. ***Meetings, processes, and roles:*** *We will meet once per week through video conference, and in person once per month, one week ahead of the capstone project's milestone assignments due dates. Each member is required to attend unless there is an emergency. If possible, please give the group at least twenty-four hours' notice if you cannot attend a meeting. Each member will be assigned a role for each formal meeting (to record action items, lead the discussion, keep time, etc.). All team members must actively contribute to discussion and work. Documents will be shared through our school's cloud service.*

3. *Accountability and dispute resolution:* *All members are expected to treat each other with respect. If there's a disagreement, members will discuss the matter directly first, and if no resolution is possible, will ask for help from the rest of the team. If the team has an impasse, the team will go as a group to the professor to ask for help in arbitrating the matter.*

4. *Celebration and customs:* *At the end of the semester, we will hold a family potluck picnic to celebrate all of our hard work. This event will be planned together, with everyone pitching in equally. For in-person team meetings, each member will rotate the job of bringing gluten-free sweets for everyone to enjoy.*

Conflict resolution checklist

Here are some tips based on Christine's years of experience as a leadership development expert and professional executive coach, which can be used for interactions at school, work, and home to prevent conflict from escalating and to manage conflict while you're in it.

Twelve strategies for effective conflict resolution

☐ **Acknowledge the problem**
(Identify that a problem exists and that it needs to be addressed.)

☐ **Listen and respond with an empathy statement that names the emotion**
(Reduce the impact of each emotion, being calm as needed.)

☐ **Maintain and enhance self-esteem**
(Demonstrate caring for the other person at every opportunity, focus on strengths not weaknesses.)

☐ **Confront issues and behaviours, not personalities or values**
(Focus on the facts, not the feelings, and work through one issue at a time.)

☐ **Discuss the conflict privately**
(Meet on neutral ground, keep the issue private until it has been discussed and or resolved.)

☐ **Use caution with words**
(Use "I" statements to help de-personalize the conflict, focus on the issue, and avoid placing blame.)

☐ **Be positive and direct**
(Say what you mean in a clear and factual manner. Focus on what can be done versus what can't be done. Focus on the future, not the past.)

☐ **Be curious**
(Seek to understand versus be understood; ask questions and don't assume; pay attention to body language. This will help you find common ground and understand the other person's perspective.)

- [ ] **Seek a win-win solution**
  (Co-create ideas and be willing to compromise. Quickly clear which issues are negotiable and which are not.)

- [ ] **Accept and appreciate personality differences**
  (Even though conflict that stems from differences in personalities can be tough, each person brings a unique perspective that merits consideration.)

- [ ] **Keep things in perspective**
  (Reflect on the true implications of the conflict. Ask yourself if this will matter to you in a few days or weeks. Adjust your position accordingly.)

- [ ] **Remain objective and effusive**
  (Be aware of defensiveness and subjectivity in order to foster an open and collaborative conflict-resolution process. Instead, be gracious and heartfelt, showing your gratitude for the conversation.)

Putting conflict resolution in action, from the executive coach, Christine:

First, I invite you to shift any preconceived notions about conflict being negative. Conflict can be healthy and actually increase the strength of the outcome. When conflict is focused on facts and not feelings, it can stimulate meaningful discussion and debate, generate new and diverse ideas, all for the better of the intended outcome.

That said, we realize that for many, conflict is not fun, and it can be difficult to engage in. It's often easier to retreat versus actively resolve an issue. During an MBA program, conflict is possible and can be triggered by the accelerated pace of learning, sheer volume of deliverables, and pressure of working in a team of peers who each have different objectives for the program, calibre of work, and total contribution levels.

The most common type of conflict experience in an MBA program is that of team dispute. Not all programs do a great job of allocating teams to create adequate diversity or blend the students based on quality of contribution and/or potential participation levels. Conflict can appear when a team member over-relies on the remainder of the group to bring them along for the ride. Say, for example, when the member uses others to fill a skill gap without contributing their strengths equally. When this happens, many students are unsure of how to proceed. They don't want to disturb the group's dynamics or jeopardize their success, but they also feel conflicted about giving someone a free ride in the program.

The conflict-resolution tips provided have been a refreshing starting point for students in these experiences. Use them to get grounded into the reality at play and to depersonalize the issue. The conflict resolution checklist provides a place to start because you must address the issue. Ultimately, the free-rider problem is one that cannot be avoided and is exactly the kind of thing you'll be expected to be able to handle as a leader. The more you practice the skill of embracing conflict as a mechanism to produce favourable outcomes, the better you will be at it.

The other time we see conflict appear in an MBA program is when there are opposing opinions present that are irreconcilable. It is certainly common that a dominant personality disposition is drawn to an MBA program (call it Type A, drivers, reds, etc.), and those kinds of people can get to a point where there's a clash quite easily. We know this firsthand because both Renée and I have strong personalities, too. We all like to be in charge and correct, and the reality is that not all of us can be in charge and correct all of the time. When this kind of conflict happens, it's great to *practice actively listening and to reference the conflict resolution tips to remove the emotion and respond objectively. Again, these are the kinds of skills that will serve you well beyond your MBA and practicing them in a school environment is a good skill builder.*

First semester and throughout the program: Hold step-through meetings

If we told you that sixty to seventy percent of MBAs who do this one thing early in their MBA program end up with expanded relationships that benefit them significantly, would you do it? Would you give this one thing a try if it increased job satisfaction as a result of contributing more strategically to the organization? This one thing is probably out of your comfort zone, but we recommend that out of the comfort zone is exactly where you need to be to demonstrate your development and growing capabilities as you work through the program. The best time to get started is right away. Don't wait until the program is over to start getting the most of your MBA investment and experience.

The one thing we're talking about that makes such a difference in post-graduation results and experience during the MBA is what we call the "step-through meeting", which is a series of meetings with you and a senior leader who is two levels above you in the organizational hierarchy. This concept was created by Christine in an effort to help MBA (and non-MBA) clients communicate effectively up through an organization on anything from program ROI to gaining a better understanding of the overall business. Step-through meetings are held in the range of every four to eight weeks and are just forty-five minutes long.

Even if your employer is not paying for your program, having step-through meetings demonstrates your commitment to growing within the company and sharing what you've been learning. This time with someone of influence a few levels more senior than you also allows for you to demonstrate your ability to think bigger and your capacity to do more than you are currently doing. It also creates space for discussion about your career with the organization when the time is right. If it seems awkward to book a meeting with a leader who is two levels above you, consider the importance of connecting with someone who has a greater level of insight into the future of the business, its resourcing needs, and where you could fit. And consider that this person probably knows the least about you, yet if selected accurately, could probably be the most helpful to your career.

Often, students assume because they've gone through the process to consider, apply, and commit to doing an MBA, their employer recognizes that they want to evolve their career and knows about their development aspirations. But are your leaders fully aware that you want to develop and grow? Have you stated your aspirations? What may be obvious to you might be completely unknown to others, and you must be explicit and strategic in sharing your goals with the people around you who can make those goals become reality.

In fact, in many cases, employers may assume that your development has been taken care of for the duration of the program and they don't need to invest the time in you for now. They may even pass you over for a promotion because they think you're too busy. You may already be fit for the next level or position and ready and willing to take on a new challenge, but missing the opportunity because you've left these aspirations unsaid. Assuming your leader knows about your career objectives is a risky assumption to make. We encourage you to be sure you are crystal clear about what you want.

Ask yourself if those who need to know about your aspirations are fully aware of what they look like. If your answer is that they should be, or they must surely know, there's potential you haven't been clear enough, and we encourage you to have an explicit conversation with an influential leader right away.

Action tip:
booking your step–through meetings

1. Identify the step-through leader

Choose a leader who is respected, has high credibility, is valued for their formidable reputation, and who holds a senior-level position that is two levels above you in your organization's hierarchy.

When looking for this leader, think like a consumer. Much like an online review where you may look for a rating for a restaurant or a real-life product experience, source the crowd around you to find a leader who has what you're looking for. Begin by asking around in a friendly and soft way about the people you're considering. What's it like working for this person? What are they known for? What would you recommend them for? Be curious and ask open-ended questions that allow you to gauge the quality of conversation, leadership, and focus you can expect from this leader.

You could meet with someone in your business group or department, which is advantageous if you want to stay in that area. If you want to pivot to another area, seek out another leader in an area of interest. Leaders who hold MBAs will often easily say yes to a request for a step-through meeting because they've likely been in your shoes. Use the classic influence principle of similarity to get a meeting with a fellow MBA.

Where we've seen leader selection go wrong is when students choose someone without a strong reputation, but someone they get along with well personally and may know very well already. If there's a strong bond there, the senior leader and the student could be seen as sharing one identity where both personal brands are tied together negatively. Ultimately, you want to forge your own path ahead and redefine who you are in your organization and career. If there's a risk of an alliance being formed with a negative perception that may impact your future, look for other leaders and find out as much information as you can about the leader ahead of time.

2. Talk to your current leader and get their support

Your goal here is to involve your current leader in the process but not have them attend your meeting with the senior leader. Ideally, these are to be one-to-one meetings with you and the senior leader.

Start by letting your leader know what these meetings are and that they're about demonstrating the value of the investment in the program and your development to a leader you don't already know. This holds true whether the investment is yours or the organization is paying for your MBA. You can even say that the reason you're setting up these meetings is because this book recommended you should and that you consider it part of your program (which we believe in strongly, and so we are happy to take the blame for your request).

Share that the value of these meetings comes from assuming the great relationship that is already established with your direct leader, and this is about building new relationships and positioning yourself differently within the company because your aspirations are to grow within your organization. By meeting with a different leader, you'll be able to see a different picture, different concepts, and a total view of the organization.

Your boss might not have an MBA. They may feel anxious about this request or intimidated. Consider these possibilities and manage your direct leader well so they continue to see your MBA studies and future as positive endeavours. You want to be assertive, but not overly aggressive. Ultimately, you will need your direct leader to advocate for you in the short term if your chosen senior leader asks why they should accept this meeting with you, and in the long term for any future job opportunities.

Your direct leader may ask to come to the meeting with you for a variety of reasons. Time with senior leaders is valuable and many are threatened by that. The risk of your direct leader joining these meetings is that your boss will look to equally contribute during the meeting to hold their spot in the room and their position generally. This can quickly turn the situation political, whereas by keeping the meeting to just you and the senior leader, you create a space where you're having a focused conversation on your development. These meetings are about you, so be confident enough to ask for that. In a one-on-one setting, the senior leader can ask you questions, challenge you, and uncover what this experience means for you at a deeper level. It also gives you the space to speak freely about your development and challenges.

The purpose of the step-through meetings is self-serving in nature (which is not the dreadful thing actions taken for the self often get made out to be), so we recommend that you go alone. Just remember, no one is going to look out for your career as well as you can for yourself, and that all other successful individuals were in a similar position at one time and can therefore empathize and relate with what you're trying to do. However, only you know the situation you find yourself in and perhaps your direct leader carries so much influence that it's best to include them, or perhaps it's just not worth the hassle to exclude them.

Regardless of whether your boss wants to attend the meeting or not, you can also share your agenda and notes with your direct leader and offer to have a debriefing about the conversations you had. Taking this one step further, you can offer to co-create your agenda with your direct leader, drawing on what you're doing and the current situation at work and in the organization. By letting them help coach you on how to position your step-through meeting, you get some extra leadership time and you're including everyone. Plus, this gives your leader an important opportunity to contribute to your success.

3. Reach out to the step-through leader of choice

Start the conversation with a phone call or casual conversation to set the intent of the request, and follow up with an email. If you haven't already made a connection with this leader's executive assistant, do that right away. Executive assistants are essential to making these meetings a success, as they are to most things that happen in an organization. Be warm and genuine, establishing a long-term relationship where you can outline what you need, the process for the meetings, and how they can help.

4. Schedule the series of meetings

Demonstrate your commitment to holding these meetings regularly and schedule the whole series from the start. Aim to meet once every four to eight weeks for the duration of the program for forty-five minutes each meeting, which will give your leader time to get to their next meeting and not feel rushed in their time with you. Include the agenda in the meeting request, and the information that the agenda is built on are the courses you're taking at the time and what you're learning in each. For each course, note how you're applying new knowledge and perspective to your current role or the opportunities that you see to apply it further or in other areas of the business. The key here is to link your studies to your work and/or organization.

A sample step-through meeting agenda

1. **Operations management |** Discuss critical-path methodology and potential application to the supply chain process

2. **Human resources and organizational behaviour |** Discuss enterprise-wide engagement strategy, observations, and senior leadership sponsorship of action-planning process

3. **Managerial accounting** | Discuss rationale for not having an activity-based costing accounting practice at the business-unit level and the opportunities that may exist

4. Etc.

5. Etc.

What you'll get from step-through meetings and how you'll know they're working

At a very minimum, the step-through meetings will help you demonstrate your growing capability and build a relationship with a leader. You will increase your presence with your current employer, gaining some vertical exposure (with those higher than you in the organizational hierarchy), which may be quite a departure from your current role. Ideally, you've shifted the perception from the person you've always been toward what you will be, with a view to all the work you're doing behind the scenes to grow and develop. This exposure sets some incredible things in motion.

The meetings will slowly but surely evolve to productive conversations around what's next for you and your career development. You'll know they are going well when they don't get cancelled. Often, we hear from senior leaders how much they enjoy these meetings and that they quickly become a priority for them. As the conversation evolves, you can mention things like where your current role doesn't allow you to apply what you're learning and know it's OK to be open about that. If the leader doesn't know specifically what an application opportunity looks like, they can't help you.

We also hear a lot from clients about how these meetings help fuel capstone or major projects, which are a common component of MBA programs. If you have an idea for a capstone project, discuss it with your senior leader right away – don't wait for the capstone or major project class to get the ideas flowing. A capstone project may also be the perfect way to contribute something meaningful to a business area outside of the one you currently work in.

Renée's experience with step-through meetings:

I asked my vice-president at the time for my step-through meetings, and like many, was a bit nervous to do so. He was very enthusiastic in his initial response, which was reassuring, but I was pleasantly surprised by his level of engagement and focus in all our meetings. Quite quickly, he took it as a point of pride that I was the only one he knew who was bringing my learning back to the organization. He loved the format of going through each course and hearing what I was learning, and soon asked to add a bullet point to our agenda on how all of this was changing me as a human being. Our conversations were lively, and he was curious about everything. I also found this process an important reflection on what I was learning and invaluable to helping me articulate the skills I was picking up. This vice-president remains an important advocate for me.

Chapter 6
Maintaining skills: Fulfilling your intention beyond graduation

Fulfilling your intention for all that you want from your MBA beyond graduation takes focus and dedication. In this chapter, you'll find our best practical tips to help you do just that. They include foundational exercises like breathing and articulating what you're best at, some templates to record your progress, all you need to make an instant credibility statement and more. This is also the chapter where you learn when to use the MBA letters.

Connect to your mind and begin with intention

If mindfulness is new, observing your breath is a good place to start connecting with your mind. You can do it wherever you are, and it's free.

Action tip:
Seventy intentional breaths a week

This may seem like an abrupt start to this chapter, and it is so intentionally. We wholeheartedly believe that getting grounded and centred through focused breathing is a required foundation to being aware, open, and intentional. This is particularly true for you, our reader, as you are likely always busy, distracted, and dealing with many competing priorities that impact your ability to be present. To get started building this as a practice, block time in your calendar to just breathe deeply for ten breaths (a full inhale and exhale for each count) each day for one week. Your task is simply to follow your breath and observe. You can do this while driving, sitting in your office with the door closed, waiting in line, or listening to a lecture in the classroom. Truly, this can be done anywhere, and it only takes a few minutes. We know the skill of connecting with your mind by reducing distractions through breathing will be extremely helpful while in an MBA program and in your life beyond.

At the end of the week, record how observing your breath impacted your week. What's different from when you began? How did it feel?

Even a minimal time commitment to being with your breath on purpose can make a noticeable difference to your day.

Mohammed's experience with seventy intentional **breaths a week:** Because Mohammed is immersed in a highly technical world at work, the thought of putting any of his limited time toward simply breathing seemed like a waste of his time. *"I honestly don't feel I have time to focus on just breathing when I have assignments, work, and family commitments to focus on,"* shared Mohammed. *"What is the clear outcome here? How can this help me get better grades?"*

We reminded Mohammed of his goal to expand his strategic abilities beyond the technical realm and into the qualitative aspects needed for leadership and for course-specific challenges like presenting his ideas in front of a group. Breathing helps focus intention and calm, which Mohammed needs. Mohammed agreed to try this action tip and recorded his thoughts in a desktop spreadsheet.

"I felt silly at first. I decided to do the breaths in the car while I waited for my kids after soccer practice. At the end of the week, I had to do a presentation in our human resources class, which is a subject I'm struggling with. When I read my classmates' feedback of my presentation, several people noted I spoke more clearly and slowly than I had in other presentations. My kids also said that I was more relaxed by Friday, even though they were slow rounding up their equipment. So I'm not sure I saw it the first few days, but slowing down to take a few breaths each day ended up with me showing up differently at school and with my kids. That was a small amount of effort to get a few key results."

Uniquely you –
articulating what you're best at

Learning what your skills are and becoming comfortable in articulating them are arguably some of the most challenging and rewarding practices we can do. We're not used to singling out our unique capabilities. If we are good at knowing what our strongest capabilities are, it's often challenging to put them into words. Sometimes, we just hope that others know what we're good at.

The reality is that most people won't know what you're good at until you tell them. Even if they did know, why would you take their word over yours? When we can articulate what we're good at, we create a shift in our belief that we can do other things. You can be something different than what you've always been. Changing your professional identity is one of the biggest transformation opportunities in the MBA experience. The first job is finding out and convincing yourself of what's possible with your unique skillset before you can start to articulate this with confidence.

The model below will help you figure out what you're best at and articulate the themes of your unique skillset. The focus here is on your transferrable skills – those that you exhibit regularly and have strength in, which have helped you to create success in the past. Transferrable skills are not job specific or technical. They are the building blocks for the next iteration of what you are in your professional life. Often, transferrable skills can be more leadership oriented. It's about how you get the work you do done. Essentially, your transferrable skills are what make you successful. They are totally unique to you, blending together in a recipe that's all yours.

At the most basic level, your transferrable skills describe what you're good at. What are you known for? What would your network of colleagues, clients, and other contacts say about you? How would people answer the question, "What is Jane exceptionally good at?"

The model has three simple questions to help you to identify what your skills are:

- **What are you most proud of?** Think of your most successful career moments from the past three to five years. Recency is important, and try to stick to career-focused moments but it's OK to include a personal moment if it's a strong example.

- **What did you do to enable that success?** This is not about your team, boss, or the collective work of which you've been a part. This is about you. We are taught that our success comes through the work of others and that which we accomplish with others. While that's true for many situations, this is one exception in which you need to focus on yourself exclusively. It might feel uncomfortable, but focus on what you did to contribute to the success that stands out to you. If you're really stuck on the team effort, reflect on how your contributions make a team effective.

- **What skills were required for that situation?** List the specific skills you exhibited in each example of a success you're most proud of. Finding this hard? It is the hardest step. Try talking this through with a trusted colleague or someone familiar with the situation who can help you look at your contributions objectively.

Here's an example of how one accomplishment moves through the model:

Most proud – Joining an organization where my business unit had the lowest engagement scores across the organization. Within in two years, I took those scores to the second highest in the company.

What did you do? – I took the feedback from the survey, read all of it, and put it into themes. I brought it back to the team where I got more feedback on the themes, and then checked in monthly on the progress being made on the issues.

Skills – Listening (I truly listened to what my team was saying), analytical (I assessed the results and discerned the key points), influential (my team wanted to follow along with me on our progress at the monthly check-ins and respected me enough to do it), motivational (the team was inspired with our results and progress)

The beautiful thing about this model is that as you go through multiple examples of your most proud accomplishments, you will find themes in your successes that you can take as your transferrable skills. Articulating your transferrable skills also ties in nicely with your instant credibility statement, which you'll create and practice next.

Action tip:
Identify your transferrable skills

Use this tool to identify and articulate your transferrable skills. Be patient with yourself and take the time you need to look at each event you're most proud of in order to draw out what your unique skills are.

What are you most proud of?	What did you do to enable that success?	What skills were required for that situation?
Example: Moved my team's engagement scores from 65% to 83% in one year	• Gathered feedback from the team • Ensured each team member's perspective was heard • Facilitated a discussion to create alignment on team norms • Created a plan for execution of changes and delivered on that plan	• Active listening • Motivating others • Influence • Strategic thinking

What are you most proud of?	What did you do to enable that success?	What skills were required for that situation?
Example 2		
Example 3		
Example 4		
Example 5		
Example 6, etc.		

The instant credibility statement

Hi. I'm someone you're going to remember.

As the saying goes, you never get a second chance to make a first impression. As a potential MBA student, a recently graduated MBA student, or seasoned MBA professional, you're looking to meet new people and find new opportunities. Chances are also good that the way you've been introducing yourself follows the same tired format favoured by networking minglers since the dawn of the after-work drink.

It's not your fault. We're conditioned to introduce ourselves this way. "Hi, I'm Renée. I'm a director of communications. What do you do?" We've all done it, and it's basically the expected format on how these things should go. But there's a better way; a much better way that allows you to be remembered for the things you want to achieve rather than what you've done.

We call it the instant credibility statement, and it's about to become your new, best introduction. The goal is to create a simple and succinct way to introduce yourself that's meaningful and memorable. A credibility statement can be thirty seconds or three minutes long, and we generally recommend aiming for a statement that is about a minute long.

Mastering your credibility statement so you can deliver it smoothly for your next meeting, networking event, or job interview requires some focused prep work and lots of practice. Let's get shaking hands and meeting your future. After all, the only way to help people understand what you're capable of is to tell them.

Building your instant credibility statement

The instant credibility statement formula has been in use for more than a decade and was created by Christine for executive coaching clients who were looking to make career and leadership pivots. For most, they had always been one thing in their career lives and were looking to be something else or to do something else. They wanted to be seen in a new way. The credibility statement allows you to introduce yourself so you're remembered the way you want to be remembered, and it all happens in an instant, effectively establishing yourself differently than you may have done in the past.

We all know how to introduce ourselves based on what we've done, but it's much harder to introduce yourself based on where you want to go, particularly if you don't yet know where you want to go. That's why we'll focus on your skills to create conversations that turn into opportunities.

When we introduce ourselves based on the career we have, especially during networking events or in a business setting (though it happens at casual gatherings, too), and when we anchor what we're saying to our pasts, we're missing an opportunity. The same-old introduction could be made much stronger by articulating your transferrable skills and leaving the person you're talking to wanting more. More importantly, you're shaping how the person will remember you.

The instant credibility statement includes:

- Who you are
- What you do
- Why you love what you do
- Why the other person should care (What's in it for the person you're meeting?)

Who you are

Be conscious about how you begin, starting with your name and talking about how you fit into the setting. You can use your title if you want, but you don't have to. Include any important identifiers that make you different from anyone else. It's important to link who you are with the context of the place. Are you at a networking event? Presentation? Social gathering? One-on-one interview? Establish early who you are and your spot in the room.

Jessica, at a marketing conference:

"Hi there, I'm Jessica. Wow, that last presenter really spoke to me on how design can transform people's moods."

Jessica doesn't use her title or credentials here, but focuses on her enthusiasm and identifies herself as a person interested in design and its impact. For context on why they are speaking with each other, she directly references the presentation she and the other person just attended.

What you do

This could be your job title, or what you do in terms of the skills you deliver. Preferably, you want to lead with your skills rather than your current title to establish how you want to be viewed.

Jessica, at a marketing conference:

"When I work with clients to create apps that drive high sales, I'm focused on listening to what their business is really about so that I can pick up the emotional details. I use those details

*to create online spaces that customers enjoy spending time on
and will ultimately enjoy spending their money on, too."*

Jessica highlights here some of her top transferable skills:
listening, emotional intelligence, strategic design, and
delivering measurable results. She keeps her comments
in line with the topic of the conference presentation by
linking back to how it feels to work with her and to visit
one of her apps.

Why you love what you do

This is the piece that makes you memorable. The meaning you
find in your work is unique to you, as is your one-of-a-kind
perspective. Your statements could include:

"…enables me to use my MBA-level education daily…"

"I enjoy what I do because I'm able to make a meaningful
impact on others…"

"I find great satisfaction in pulling many pieces together
to build the big picture…"

Think of this piece as an opportunity to bring in your education without sounding overly confident or arrogant (always
a reminder worth keeping at the forefront). This is a safe
way to talk about your education and experience subtly. You
could also include your North Star in this or link your passion
to your strongest skillset. Most importantly, be genuine in
your enthusiasm.

Jessica, at a marketing conference:

"It's really energizing and rewarding for me to be able to see my clients' businesses represented digitally in a way that honours their customers. What a great bonus to know that my ten years of design experience and related education can change people's moods positively, too!"

In closing, Jessica conveys her passion for delivering results to clients and how she loves to make customers happy. Again, she keeps her comment tied to the conference presentation about moods.

Why they should care

Your goal here is to send the conversation over to the person you're meeting to demonstrate your connection, invite questions, and keep the conversation going. At its simplest, you want to give the person you're meeting something interesting to talk about or to return to something you have in common.

Jessica, at a marketing conference:

"So, that's what I enjoyed, but what stood out for you with the last speaker?"

This is a short, open-ended question that creates a lot of opportunity for the person responding to say anything. Jessica's question also conveys genuine interest in getting to know what was important to another person and gives her a great opening to ask more questions to keep the conversation going.

Bringing it all together

Let's go through an example from a client who changed her introduction from standard fare to an instant credibility statement built for her next career move. Let's call this client "Sarah", a senior-level accountant working as a controller in a large organization. She felt the world was not getting the best from her, so she went back to school to get her Executive MBA while working full time in the career she has had for more than two decades. Sarah loved being a leader and was interested in becoming an HR leader and moving away from accounting entirely.

When asked to introduce herself to a potential vice-president of a human resources department, here's what she offered:

> *"Hi, I'm Sarah at XYZ organization. I have been an accountant for twenty-five years, most recently fulfilling the controller role. I have certified management accounting and certified general accounting designations as well, and I've done some finance education in the past. I have really grown up through managerial accounting and have led teams along the way. I've really enjoyed the human resources aspects of leading teams, and partnering with the HR function. I'd love to hear more about what you do and how you got to where you are today."*

Sarah wants to get a human resources role , but leads her introduction with her accounting experience. This is a natural tendency of how we usually define ourselves, but leaves out what we are learning or know and what we are currently doing. But look what happens when she shifts the first two sentences or so to be about where she's moving toward instead of where she's been. She focuses on telling a story about how accounting has led her to develop leadership skills:

> *"Hi, my name is Sarah. I'm a leader who has grown through the ranks of my organization. I have had strong success in motivating teams of high performers and delivering exceptional results on tight deadlines and within budget. I have a background in accounting, I've dabbled in finance, and I'm currently studying business. What I enjoy about the leadership side of business is that I can capture my passion for making an impact on people and work with the human resources team to increase employee engagement and drive culture. I appreciate the opportunity to meet with you today. What are the ways your organization is increasing employee engagement?"*

Sarah's second introduction is significantly different. It's still the same true story, but the angle of the story is different. She's chosen what she wants to highlight and is intentional about how she positions herself. This is an exceptionally important skill when it comes to navigating successful career transitions.

Here are two more examples from Mohammed, who is in the middle of his MBA journey, and Leena, who has already completed her MBA.

Mohammed, at an informational coffee chat with someone he believes can help him to land a leadership role:

> *"Hello, I'm Mohammed. Thanks for taking the time to connect. Our friend Peter says you're the best at leading diverse teams within complex technical environments. I'm currently in a complex environment myself as I pursue my*

MBA. I've been focusing my leadership within our diverse teams on how I can help my classmates implement strategy and work best together. I'm learning that the strongest results come from watching for and applying the qualitative parts of the strategy, not just the numbers, and I've been enjoying using my critical thinking and empathy skills to do just that. It's been fun to solve problems with people and gain a different perspective of how people work. What do you focus on when you lead technical teams?"

Mohammed could have easily told this person that they're both mechanical engineers, but instead has focused his introduction on what he hopes to be – a leader, and not just a technical expert. He is also highlighting his learning mentality and that he is focused on the people side of getting work done. Mohammed is letting this person know he's ambitious and wants to learn from the other person's experience. This is a great start to a productive conversation about where Mohammed is going rather than where he's been.

 Leena, at a professional event talking to someone outside of her current network:

"Hi there. I'm Leena, it's nice to meet you. I'm a leader focused on broad, organizational strategy. I love what I do because my work allows me to lead others and build strong relationships, and that means I am able to achieve results beyond my technical areas of expertise, with my team and for the organization. I look at both the people on my teams and the organization holistically, and that means I can use my skills and Master of Business Administration degree to think across all aspects of our strategy for maximum impact.

> *Since joining this group, I've learned a lot from other leaders on the strategies we need to grow thriving companies in the challenging economic times ahead and am happy to share! What brings you here?"*

Leena's updated instant credibility statement starts with her capabilities as a leader and her most important skills. Her statement also signals she's interested in growing her network by creating mutual benefit and exchanging ideas with the new people she's meeting. She's clear in stating her ambition to lead at the highest levels of a company and has positioned herself as someone who works with others effectively through strong relationships. Most importantly, Leena is making her story known outside of her company.

Strength in versions and practice

You can, and should, have many different versions of your credibility statement. You can't approach each meeting the same way, and there are at least seven business-related situations you should have a statement ready for. Aiming toward your goals should always be an intentional part of your conversations, highlighting what's relevant in each encounter you find yourself in.

1. Networking events
2. MBA events, in the classroom
3. Presentations, conferences, important meetings
4. Meetings with senior-level leaders
5. Interviews
6. Informational interviews (such as coffee chats)

7. Social events

Delivering your credibility statement smoothly and more naturally becomes easier as you practice. Write your statements down and say them aloud. You can even say them in front of a mirror or during the commute to work.

Deliver your credibility statement with passion and conviction. While that may sound obvious, don't take for granted that your energy needs to be felt by others. If you're not interested in and excited about what you're saying, why would anyone else be? Keep your credibility statement succinct. Avoid blabbing on about where you were born, your first pet, etc. This isn't your life story; it's just a captivating opener to have a meaningful conversation. Be respectful of your audience's time and leave the person wanting more and asking questions of you.

Lastly, remember there are two people in any conversation, so listening is critical. Active listeners show respect, pay attention, and find ways to consider fully what another is saying. Ask open-ended questions, show genuine interest, and be involved with each person you meet.

Action tip:
Build your own instant credibility statement

Start your first instant credibility statement here, and build additional versions using this format. Practice and practice until the format is memorized. Be succinct (but not rushed) and present with conviction and passion to leave a positive lasting impression.

The instant credibility statement template

1. Who you are (name and other important identifiers)

2. What you do (your role, profession, some relevant specifics)

3. Why you love it (include your experience and credentials, if applicable)

4. Why the other person should care (What's in it for the person you're meeting?)

___

My instant credibility statement, draft one

___

My instant credibility statement, draft two

MBA: When to use the letters

Once you've earned your Masters of Business Administration, one of the next challenges MBAs face is how to use these credentials in the best way possible. For some MBA graduates, the question lingers for years. When do you use them? When don't you? What are the implications of adding "MBA" to your various professional profiles and in conversation?

We use our credentials to build credibility. At the most basic level, it's naming credit for what you've earned. It sounds simple but gets complicated when you use your MBA credentials and see someone back away or react negatively. There's a risk in overdoing the credit. What we want to avoid in using MBA credentials is coming across as arrogant, too bold, or aggressively ambitious. Like it or not, there's a perception that MBAs are all of the above, and that can make others feel threatened. It's a common view that MBAs are out to take over the world. You will also encounter many people who just don't value graduate degrees, MBA degrees in particular. Most MBAs we know want to avoid this perception and don't want to be seen as arrogant, bold, or aggressively ambitious either.

There are just three letters, MBA, but they can appear to hold more than the acronym abbreviates, and it's something to be mindful of in your communications. We're not advocating that you become a silent part of the wallpaper. Rather, using your credentials wisely is about being mindful, observant, and strategic – it's an active stance and not a passive one. So, when can you use MBA? Once again, the answer is that it depends.

Using your MBA credentials in various formats, or choosing not to, comes down to knowing your audience and the purpose of your communication. Knowing your audience means considering the context, including the culture of the company and society that you're in.

Certain industries and companies value advanced education highly, and MBAs in particular. Learn quickly if these things are valued by others around you, inside and outside your company. Does your company hire for new recruits based on education? Do key leaders in your organization have MBAs or other advanced degrees? And if so, do they put them in their email signatures? If it's not common to use MBA or other designations where you work, don't do it. Read the internal environment and follow the lead of others. If you're unsure, ask a business partner in the human resources area about the culture of using MBA credentials.

Also consider who you interact with in your role. If you're outward facing, the context may be different with respect to clients and customers than it is with your executive team. What are your clients looking for? What do they need to know to trust you? It's important to navigate the assumptions in all of your environment and to be sure of your audience. In the case of email signatures, consider having two or more versions to use as appropriate.

If you're a consultant, we recommend that use your credentials always. Your information is easily forwarded and shared in a consultancy kind of environment, and having your MBA associated with you is simply good for referrals (which you can't predict or follow all of the time). Best to be prepared across all channels.

When it comes to business cards, we are generally a big yes for including MBA. You never know where a business card is going to go, and complete information is best. If there was anywhere to have your MBA written down, the real estate of the business card is the place to do it because it demonstrates commitment. However, keep in mind the analog nature of this medium. The business card is antiquated in many contexts, but the audience that cares about business cards might be exactly the audience that wants to see your credentials. Consider too the importance of business cards in different cultures.

With today's technology, it's the digital environment where most peers, bosses, and customers will find your profile and that trend is not likely to decrease. Whether you include your MBA credentials will depend on the particular environment and the purpose of your communications, just like in real life. Your personal Facebook page is wholly different from your LinkedIn page, which is wholly different from your company's Twitter feed or WeChat site. Each should have a different purpose and specific considerations on how you portray yourself professionally.

For LinkedIn profiles, we are a yes to including your MBA credentials. This site is dedicated to showcasing your education and work experience, so this information absolutely belongs there. Can you use MBA at the end of your name or in your summary statement sub-headline? Generally, yes, because it helps with searches by recruiters. As always, consider if your purpose is to be found by a recruiter and if having MBA in your name might help a recruiter to find you more easily. As a witty fellow MBA once joked, "Where's the best place to hide a dead body? Page two of the search results. No one goes there."

Whether you're including your MBA credentials or talking about having an MBA, it's important to talk about the results and not just the letters. For example, you could share something like, "I did a case study once where I discovered how easy it is to succumb to group think in times of crisis, so I'd like to suggest we pause right now to see if we're in danger of doing that, because I want us to get the best possible outcome here."

You're not saying you have an MBA here, but you're directly applying what you've learned and you've done it in a way that's considerate of others and the goals you share. Bringing in a better environment and results for everyone works to safely introduce your MBA background because it's not all about you. It's always best to link your experience to the performance of the business and of other people, without just listing off credentials. Think more about demonstrating and less on the telling.

How often you talk about having your MBA will be different for everyone. Some people find it easy; others find it quite difficult. Some people are actively discouraged from talking about it at work, particularly if they are one of the few who have been supported financially through an MBA and others haven't had the opportunity. Use your best judgement if there are political considerations in play.

Remember too that you can create a safe environment to talk about all the MBA subjects you want by staying connected with your cohorts and your MBA network. We highly recommend reaching out to discuss the things you find interesting and keep all that you learned fresh with someone who comes from a shared experience with you. Your network can be an incredible sounding board on a wide range of things, especially on what you might need to consider when using your MBA credentials in a particular environment.

Intentional practices for maximizing your investment

Here are a few extra tools and habits to help you on your journey.

Daily intention scorecard

This daily reflection is designed for busy people and helps assess how balanced your life is in the way you run it and to identify any gaps when it comes to being your best self. You can change anything on the left column to suit your goals or areas of focus. For example, you may want to include things like family time, self-care, education, work, etc. This reflection practice allows you to be more conscious about potential deficits in any given area by giving you a quantitative measure. The awareness you gain will foster space for choice and intention to address any deficits (or surpluses). Solidify the habit and set a daily reminder in your calendar to do this.

The daily intention scorecard

Score one to five on how successful you were in accomplishing your goal in each aspect, with one being the lowest and five being the highest. The completed daily intention scorecard below provides a glimpse into a week for Mohammed.

	My Goal	Monday	Tuesday	Wednesday	Thursday	Friday	Saturday	Sunday
Leadership	Be the best leader I can be for my team	4	3	3	2	2	NA	NA
Intention and mindset	Be intentional about opportunities to build trust and relationships	5	3	3	4	4	3	3
Gratitude	Find three things I'm grateful about each day.	5	5	5	5	3	5	4
Rest	Get 7 hours of sleep.	5	2	2	2	4	5	2
Nutrition	Eat 6 small meals per day.	5	2	2	3	4	5	2
Family	Be present with my family at dinnertime.	5	5	5	1	0	5	5
School	Learn something new in school each week.	5	4	4	4	5	NA	NA
Fitness	3 x cardio and 2 x weights	0	0	5	5	5	0	5
Support (from personal support network)	Reach out to two friends per week, schedule and maintain cleaning services for the household	0	0	5	0	0	5	0
Total		34	24	34	26	27	28	21
Daily average*								
Weekly average*								

My Goal	Monday	Tuesday	Wednesday	Thursday	Friday	Saturday	Sunday
Leadership							
Intention and mindset							
Gratitude							
Rest							
Nutrition							
Family							
School							
Fitness							
Support (from personal support network)							
Total							
Daily average*							
Weekly average*							

*Track these to watch the overall trends in how you're managing your gaps. Using a spreadsheet works best.

Personal development action plan

Track your learning, increase retention, and shift your behaviour toward becoming a stronger leader with these powerful reflection and action planning questions. Add lines and dates in the style of the example provided, and keep this tracker active to help you reflect often.

Competencies and areas of focus	Action item	How (What specifically will I do?)
Example: Competency – strategic agility	Build out my personal development objectives and set goals for the people side of my business so that I not only have a strong organizational/ operational strategy, but also a people and culture strategy. Be open and aware of the importance of people as part of the strategic plan and communicate this awareness.	Create a one-page document to augment my current goals that include various installation metrics. Share these with my team and leader by DATE.

Status and/or examples (How did it go? What went well? What could be improved?)	Notes
Shared the first draft with my coach for feedback. Also shared the draft with my peer (VP HR). Went well; feedback received was valuable. VP of HR commented on how demonstrating the connection of people-related goals to the business objectives will engage team members further in understanding how they contribute to the bigger picture. Makes sense! I have a meeting scheduled with my leader for DATE to review. Will then share with my team at our weekly leadership team meeting on DATE.	Lesson learned! Presenting the big picture rationale for why I feel it's important to augment the operational strategy with a focus on the people running the business worked well. Next time, I'll spend a bit more time on sharing the full context of my plan to create openness when sharing a new approach with my leader. Continue to do this going forward. Strategy and rationale first, then the details.

Community involvement personal assessment

By weighing your options, this tool aligns your limited time with your most important intentions when it comes to volunteer opportunities. There are so many ways to help an infinite amount of causes and opportunities, but your volunteer work should also help you meet your personal and professional goals for a win-win situation. Here are a few sample goals to inspire you to make your own:

Personal goals	Professional goals
• Fulfills passion, interest, personal values • Rewarding (feels good) • Minimal time commitment (balance) • Volunteer work • Fills other personal buckets, too (fitness, family time etc.) • Different than the day-to-day • Make an impact on your neighborhood/ environment	• Networking • Skill development (leadership, finance) • Diversification (industry experience) • Opportunity to try something new • Aligned to professional interests and career path • Exposure to senior-level professionals • Paid position

Assessment

Rate each current or desired community involvement activity against your personal and professional goals, considering the criteria above and choose based on the highest score. Scores of seven or higher are generally indicative of good value for your time. This assessment provides insight into how each community involvement activity helps you fulfill your personal and professional goals.

The big question: At this point in your life, what is more important? Personal or professional interests? You can have both, but choosing activity weighted more heavily in one direction will help you accomplish what you want in that area of your life.

Community involvement activity opportunity	Ability to meet personal goals: 1 (low) – 5 (high)	Ability to meet professional goals: 1 (low) – 5 (high)	Total score
Example: Treasurer, community association board in my neighborhood	4	2	6
1.			
2.			
3.			

Go earn much more than three letters

You now have a guide to help you intentionally create your very own MBA experience. Choose to be immersed and present before, during, and for all the years that follow your MBA. You are your biggest fan and best advocate, and you have the all the tools you need to maximize your investment.

When expectation and actual experience align, remarkable things are possible. You've defined your ROI for your MBA, carefully choosing the inputs and the outcome. You've aligned your intention and purpose with your MBA experience and built a practice of habits through meaningful actions that support your ROI. You've anticipated what you might regret and planned to mitigate those things. Your effort's worth is determined by you, and we are confident that you'll do more than just earn three letters.

Keep your intentional MBA practices sharp by continuing to revisit the action tips in this guide and tracking your reflections and actions. If you know others who would benefit from the same experience, please refer this book to them. As we all know, the decision to pursue an MBA, the effort to get the most from it while in it, and the desire to leverage it for the future is not easy, and *The Intentional MBA* is here to help.

Finally, we're proud of you for considering your MBA so thoughtfully. You are going to be that shining example of the intentional MBA who stands out from the crowd and achieves all you set out to achieve. We are grateful that, through this book, we could be part of your journey. Wishing you the best MBA experience and many happy, long-lasting returns.

About the Authors

Christine Dagenais, MBA, is the Founder and CEO of Bright Wire, a premier leadership development and executive coaching firm, a professionally certified coach (PCC), and holds other industry leading credentials. Christine has worked extensively with hundreds of business leaders at all levels, with and without MBAs. She's ignited by inspiring learning in others, and helping people fulfill their potential.

Renée Francis, MBA, is a strategic communications leader living and working in San Francisco, California. For more than a decade, Renée has worked with leaders at all levels to tell corporate stories to employees, customers, and investors to get results and build trust. Driven by adventure and learning, Renée is passionate about connecting people to business.